Management Mastery and Practice Series

Ubuntu Coaching and Connection Practices for Leader-Managers

Endorsements

It is an honour for me to write a brief endorsement for your magnificent book. I thank you with my whole heart for inviting me. And I thank you for the gift to me of your inclusion of the Thinking Environment in your philosophy and framework. I am very moved. The challenge, therefore, is not what to say in my endorsement, but how to keep it short. I have learned so much, felt such connection with you, Dumi, and such gratitude for the eloquent and heart-centred voice of you as author, demonstrating precisely your key points. To be as author the very thing you espouse in the writing is a rare achievement. You have greeted me. You have seen me. You have done as an author the things you propose leaders do with the members of their teams. To read your book is to grow, to emerge a better human being and a more valuable leader. I could write for an hour about all of that. But in painfully few words: Take this book home. Savour it. Let it accompany you. It is a treasure.

– Nancy Kline, author of The Promise That Changes Everything: I Won't Interrupt You and Time To Think: Listening to Ignite the Human Mind, and Founding Director of Time To Think Ltd, UK

The world is becoming smaller, more accessible, we say. And yet, we still have so much to learn as a collective. Learn from approaches, and philosophies other than our own. If only we stay curious and open! This book by Dumisani Magadlela gives us a rare and wide invitation to explore Ubuntu, an ancient way of being and showing up. It shows up, indeed, in a powerful way in professional coaching, especially for teams. Read it – your experience will be worth it.

– Magdalena Nowicka Mook, CEO: International Coaching Federation

There are four core qualities of great leaders: compassion, curiosity, courage and connectedness. Ubuntu represents connectedness in action. That makes this book an essential read for leaders who want to grow in wisdom, and for the coaches who support them.

– Professor David Clutterbuck, Founder and Practice Lead, Clutterbuck Coaching and Mentoring International

Dumi Magadlela has long been developing approaches to coaching and leadership which reflect alternative approaches beyond Western-dominated practices. His thoughtful application of Ubuntu as a philosophy and practice has provided innovative approaches which should enable leaders in Africa to use this to grow their teams. It has applications beyond this, however, and needs to be read by those interested in teamwork across the board. The community-oriented sense of value that is inherently encompassed within his sense of connected, informed practice is inspiring. It challenges us to see the world differently, but also brings practical examples that enable its readers to apply the ideas to their own context. I thoroughly recommend it to the coaching community.

– Professor David A. Lane, Professional Development Foundation, UK

Increasingly, coaching has to transform itself from coaching individuals to coaching connections and teams. There is much we can learn from Ubuntu, which sees relationship as primary, and Dumi shows in this inspiring and practical book how Ubuntu principles can be applied not just by coaches but also by leaders. I strongly recommend it to both groups.

– Professor Peter Hawkins, Chairman of Renewal Associates, Emeritus Professor of Leadership at Henley Business School, and author of many bestselling books on coaching and leadership

This is a marvellous blend of ancient African philosophy and wisdom with modern organisational challenges, so we can all lead and manage in a more connected and human-focused way in our task-oriented and technology-dominated worlds. The book is packed full of tools, stories, examples and activities to provide the reader with practical insights and next steps. Dumi is a wonderful guide on this journey of learning.

– Dr Colm Murphy, executive coach, team coach, and partner in Praesta Ireland

It gives me goose bumps to bear witness to another building block of sharing Ubuntu with the world. As an African, Ubuntu is in my DNA. To see Ubuntu embedded in the world of work in such a practical and accessible way is a game-changer. Thank you Dr Dumi, every leader and practitioner needs a copy of your book to help them on their journey to co-creating a world we all want.

– Dr Sharon Munyaka, Organisational Psychologist

Dumisani Magadlela has written an immensely readable and practical guide for coaches and leader-managers in building effective relationships. In his deep emphasis on the power of positive connection, Dumisani honours the African practice of Ubuntu: the acknowledgement, graciously simple yet profound, that "I am because we are". He also draws on the influence of connection in Ken Wilber's Integral Vision, Daniel Goleman in his focus on emotional intelligence, and Nancy Kline for her guidelines in creating a listening culture, each of whom in their own work offers an ideal and appropriate analogy with the connectedness of Ubuntu. There are numerous practical examples of the power of positive engagement, its ability to minimise stress and enhance our innate willingness to socialise. Replete with great questions for self-reflection, Dumisani encourages the reader to explore models and practices that lead to positive engagement. Living the values and practice of Ubuntu uproots the notion of stagnant role privilege and intimidating hierarchy, and encourages instead lively, respectful connectedness across levels, where healthy relationship management can lead to dynamic productivity. The practical examples given in each chapter for teams and individuals are easy to follow. The quality of the writing and its easy readability bring to life the descriptions of models, practices and stories including some of the pitfalls to avoid. Dumisani's approach challenges a "me-first" outlook with one of collective care. This book affirms the established claim of neuroscience that we are born to socialise, and positive engagement in the way we connect brings out the best in creative thinking and collective wellbeing. With its focus on emotionally intelligent engagement, this timely book on Ubuntu coaching and the development of leader-managers touches the humanity inherently deep within us all. In this day and age, what could be more important?

– Dorrian Elizabeth Aiken PhD DProf, author of An Integral Approach to Transformative Leadership: Dancing Through the Storm

As one of the early pioneers and practitioners who has written about the importance and relevance of Ubuntu, locally and globally, Dumi Magadlela's book on Ubuntu in the context of coaching and team development is an excellent contribution to practitioners in business settings. The discourse on Ubuntu during the past three decades has tended to be theoretical and philosophical, rather than designed to help readers internalise what it means to embody Ubuntu in lived experience. The great power of this book is that it offers an accessible and practical guide for managers, coaches and team leaders. By distilling his own experience, and collecting and distilling the wisdom of others, Magadlela gives his readers valuable practical tools, tips and reflective exercises. The great gift of this book lies in its potential to enable readers to translate and apply Ubuntu values in practice.

– Barbara Nussbaum, Penguin author, award-winning social innovator, and founder and director of Finding Us in Music

Thanks, Dumi, for this timely book that integrates onboarding new leaders, enhancing self-awareness, development of Ubuntu Intelligence, and connecting with teams at a deeper level. I love the integrative exercises at the end of each chapter.

– Nobantu Mpotulo, developer and pioneer of Ubuntu Coach Training

Dr Dumisani Magadlela is a selfless African change-maker. One of the most highly-trained and well-educated leadership coaches in Africa, he maintains an attitude of curiosity, and nurtures a thirst for growth and learning that is an inspiration to me. His willingness to share his knowledge and experience in this book is a testament to his selflessness and intentionality about changing the course of Africa. Dumi has chosen to utilise his world-class coaching and leadership skills to improve African organisations and African teams, and the impact of his work can be seen and felt in countless organisations, including BCA Leadership, the pan-African coaching organisation I lead. We have been blessed to have Dumi as one of our coaches, and he continually challenges our coaches to grow and expand their knowledge and capacity. I have grown as a result of reading this book. The seven reflective questions of a leader-manager have helped me to do a personal inventory on my leadership journey. Dumi's Ubuntu vision for the world as a place where the human race operates as "one big and sometimes happy family" is not just happy talk, but a vision that drives Dumi's actions and decisions. I can personally attest to his servant-leadership that has endeared him to coaches throughout Africa and across the globe, who have elected to make him the first Chairperson of the International Coaching Federation from Africa. I encourage leaders and managers to enhance their performance through the digestion of this book; I use the word "digestion" because this book is more than a mere novel, it is a manual which can be read, reflected upon, understood, and its principles applied for enhanced leadership performance. Given the global trends of demographics persuading me that the future of the human race will be more significantly influenced by Africans, it is with delight I note that Dumi is one of the Africans taking the lead in documenting methodologies of leadership which are effective in Africa and beyond. Africa will flourish and lead the world because of African leaders like Dr Dumisani Magadlela.

– Modupe Taylor-Pearce PhD, founder and CEO of BCA Leadership

Today, the entire world runs on teams. We work in teams, and many of us work on multiple teams in a variety of ways every day. The number of teams we form, along with the complexity and diversity of those teams, has increased exponentially. There is increasing evidence that teams which share a great culture and understand each other deeply, are more likely to exceed performance expectations. Dumisani has, in this book, focused on the essential skills a manager needs to make this a reality. It's an essential read for any manager or coach.

– Michael Taylor, executive business coach and author

This is such an important work for managers and leaders in our current times, and a wonderfully pragmatic, yet deeply personalised continuation of this series. Dr Dumisani Magadlela has at the core of his heart to serve through the narrative that can resonate with our land and bring the African voice into the management and leadership landscape, while offering the universal wisdom of Ubuntu. We are often prone to using concepts that have no way to anchor themselves in the real-life landscape of application. In a world moving to further separate and compartmentalise approaches and people, the bringing together of essential parts of our humaneness into a more usable whole makes this a powerful Gestalt. Seeing humans as part of a whole system, not as disparate parts, with the common goal of becoming leaders and managers through humanising work experiences, remains at the heart and soul of the more ancient African and wisdom traditions. "I see you and all that you are" is a deep practice for each and every one of us, and in this book you receive practices to bring you closer to this. It's all about mind-sets and heart-sets: shift these into practice, and you will be and become that which is calling to you.

– Paddy Pampallis DProf, founder and CEO of The (Integral) Coaching Centre (TCC) and Integral Africa Institute, Integral scholar, and Meridian University Faculty

In quiet moments, leaders listen internally to a voice that wonders how to heal hurt, restore dignity, and ultimately sustain excellence for themselves and all those they lead, manage and serve. Fulfilling this intent takes courage, and a mind-set committed to authentic integrity rather than blindly following procedure. The spirit of Ubuntu, and the many practical skills every reader accesses in this book, are the whispers of wisdom spoken plainly and with inspiration to erase a leader's doubt.

– Janet M. Harvey, CEO of inviteCHANGE and ICF Master Certified Coach

Dedication

To Lwazi, Nobuntu, Sandile and Mosa Magadlela,
in fond memory of my two Ubuntu teachers:
my dear mother Alice Vesi Magadlela,
and my Ubuntu mentor, Mfuniselwa John Bhengu.

First published in 2023.

ISBN: 978-1-86922-997-9 (Printed)
eISBN: 978-1-86922-998-6 (PDF Ebook)

Published by KR Publishing
Tel: (011) 706-6009
E-mail: orders@knowres.co.za
Website: www.kr.co.za

Typesetting, layout and design: Cia Joubert, cia@knowres.co.za
Cover design: Marlene De Lorme, marlene@knowres.co.za
Editing and Proofreading: Nick Wilkins
Project management: Cia Joubert, cia@knowres.co.za

Management Mastery and Practice Series

Ubuntu Coaching and Connection Practices for Leader-Managers

Selected practices to grow your team in a fast-changing world

by

Dumisani Magadlela PhD

Edited by

Sunny Stout-Rostron

kr
publishing

2023

Management Mastery and Practice Series

Edited by Dr Sunny Stout-Rostron

Context

This series is suited to a range of managers. You might be a newly promoted manager or about to step into a greater managerial role with increased responsibilities. Or perhaps you have been in a management position for some years but have had no formal management training, or you are an executive leader but need to refresh your ideas on the essentials of leading and managing yourself and others. Whichever length of time you have been managing, this series is to help you deal with people management. This includes cultural diversity, systemic issues within the organisation in which you work, and to develop effective communication and coaching skills, the ability to manage conflict, difficult situations, company politics and career development.

The authors look at how to inspire staff and teams, understand motivation and demotivation, manage stress, build better performance with effective communications and well-run meetings, build great teams, and prepare leaders for the future. Each book includes theory, research, case studies, practical exercises, and tips on how to handle challenges – avoiding the pitfalls that can cause managers to fail. Your effectiveness as a leader-manager depends on what support you can expect from your staff, direct reports, and team members. This series will help you to build your skills and competence, developing your own unique signature as a leader and a manager.

Book 1: Management Mastery: Everything You Ever Wanted to Know About Managing People But Were Afraid to Ask

by Sunny Stout-Rostron and Michael Taylor with contributing author Ingra Du Buisson-Narsai

Being a leader-manager requires the skills of both management and leadership. This book covers essential aspects of both: identifying and solving your most challenging people problems quickly, and motivating your people to perform at their highest potential. Understanding when to lead and when to manage, taking a deeper dive into self-awareness and self-management, delegating to develop your team, broadening your range of communication skills in order to inspire and motivate people and managing difficult people and situations. However, the most important competence essential for stepping into being a leader-manager is that of self-awareness, conscious observation and thoroughly understanding yourself in order to lead and manage people. It is critically important that you understand and know how your teams "experience" you – because this is the path towards identifying what change is needed in terms of your own assumptions about yourself and others. It is vital to understand your own thinking, feeling and behaviour. This process is described with clear guidelines, case studies, practical exercises, and self-assessments to move you into greater competence as a leader-manager.

Book 2: Ubuntu Coaching and Connection Practices for Leader-Managers: Selected practices to grow your team in a fast-changing world

by Dumisani Magadlela, PhD

New leader-managers in the whirlwind digital world do not have the luxury of gathering all the necessary background data that will equip them with information on each member of their new team. Joining an organisation with the task of a new team, or inheriting and leading an existing one, and then growing the team to become what you envision, is a tall task at best even for the most experienced of leaders. Given the fast pace of change and access to information by many employees in the digital age, new leader-managers are faced with the daunting task of integrating the divergent views of their new team members. The task of building a high-performance team in a fast-changing digital world becomes even more complex when the new leader-manager operates from the stance of a KIA (know-it-all). Ubuntu coaching skills, ubuntu intelligence lenses, and many new tools are packed into this book to help equip new leader-managers with essential skills to become agile and versatile in a rapidly evolving environment, and to adopt an approach that helps them to build their new evolving and adaptable team. This book shares illustrative examples and easy-to-use exercises at the end of each chapter to help deepen a leader-manager's self-awareness, re-humanising a new world of work through their teams and across organisational systems.

Table of contents

Series author biographies

Sunny Stout-Rostron, DProf

An organisational development specialist, Sunny coaches at senior executive and board level. Having worked internationally in the corporate world for 20 years, she also has a wide range of experience in leadership development, helping organisations cultivate collaborative strategies to manage relationship systems, culture change and conflict. Sunny has played a leading role in building the profession of coaching and has created a succession of leadership and management programmes in the corporate, legal and educational fields. Her passion is to deepen the knowledge base for coaching through research and critical reflective practice, as well as fostering an understanding and implementation of genuine cultural diversity in organisations.

Sunny is a director of People Quotient (Pty) Ltd, a Doctoral Supervisor at several business schools, a member of the Management Coaching faculty of the University of Stellenbosch Business School (USB), part-time faculty at the South African College of Applied Psychology, and on the global faculty for Time to Think, Inc. She is a Founding Fellow at the Institute of Coaching at McLean Hospital, a Harvard Medical School Affiliate, Founding President of Coaches and Mentors of South Africa (COMENSA), and a long-standing member of the Worldwide Association of Business Coaches (WABC).

Sunny is the author of six books including: *Transformational Coaching to Lead Culturally Diverse Teams* (Routledge, 2019); *Leadership Coaching for Results: Cutting-edge practices for coach and client* (Knowres, 2014); *Business Coaching International: Transforming individuals and organisations* (Karnac 2009, 2013); and *Business Coaching Wisdom and Practice: Unlocking the secrets of business coaching* (Knowres, 2009, 2012).

Michael Taylor, MPhil

An experienced facilitator, international management consultant, and master coach, Michael has deep expertise in understanding and implementing culture change, building world-class teams and developing global leaders. He experienced first-hand the excitement of running profitable high engagement businesses, which included managing a team of 25 professional consultants. Michael is managing director of Xponential (Pty) Ltd, a professional services firm he founded in 2006, and a director of People Quotient (Pty) Ltd.

A practice leader for executive coaching and leadership development, Michael is highly regarded as a thought leader in the fields of executive coaching and team effectiveness. He has a wealth of practical experience at both management and executive levels, and inherently understands the challenges leaders face in the current world of complex volatility, uncertainty and ambiguity.

He has been instrumental in facilitating many significant global transformation projects that have seen organisations execute their strategies with greater clarity, insight and inspired leadership in diverse industries such as central banking, financial services, FMCG, information technology, digital media and telecommunications. Michael is a qualified organisational behaviourist and Master Coach and completed his MPhil in management coaching at the University of Stellenbosch Business School (USB).

Contributing author biographies

Ingra du Buisson-Narsai, MCom OrgPsych, MSc ProfPrac

Ingra is the co-founder and Director of NeuroCapital Coaching and Consulting, which consults to some of South Africa's leading and most admired companies. She has 20 years of executive-level experience in corporate South Africa, and is a Registered Organisational Psychologist in private practice. Her unique contribution is as a catalyst for change, using integrative organisational neuroscience. Ingra is also an established leadership and executive coach, and is affiliated with the Business School of the University of the Witwatersrand in South Africa, where she supervises and examines the work of postgraduate students in business and executive coaching. Ingra is an Executive Committee Member of the Society for Industrial and Organisational Psychology of South Africa (SIOPSA) and the Chair of the Interest Group of Applied Organisational Neuroscience (AONS). Ingra's academic qualifications include an MCom (Organisational Psychology), PGCNL and Master of Science (MSc) in Neuroscience of Leadership. She is busy with a PhD in Organisational Neuroscience. Ingra is the bestselling author of the newly published book *Fight, Flight or Flourish: How neuroscience can unlock human potential*. Ingra actively pursues the increasing visibility of neuroscientific methods and diagnostics in the study of organisational behaviour.

About the author

Dumisani Magadlela, PhD

Dr Dumi Magadlela is an accredited international executive coach, team coach, coach trainer, and leadership development facilitator. He has been described as an organisational "people whisperer" by some of his organisational clients.

Dumi currently works with business leaders and executives across the private, public, multi-lateral, and non-profit sectors. He has extensive experience working across the African continent and collaborating globally with other coaches and clients. He is accredited by the European Mentoring and Coaching Council as a Senior Practitioner in Team Coaching, and is working towards credentials by the International Coaching Federation (ICF), and by the Africa Board for Coaching, Consulting and Coaching Psychology (ABCCCP), as a Master Coach. 2016, Dumi was given the inaugural African Coach of the Year award by the ABCCCP. In 2021 he was shortlisted as one of the top 50 coaches in the world by the renowned Thinkers50 Group led by a leading global coach, Marshall Goldsmith.

At the time of publishing this book, Dumi was serving in the International Coaching Federation (ICF), the largest coaching body globally, as the Chairperson of the Global Enterprise Board of Directors. He is a member of the international faculty at the WBECS Global Team Coaching Institute, now Coaching.com, where he co-designs and co-facilitates team coaching training with other international faculty members. Dumi co-founded the Ubuntu Coaching Foundation at The Coaching Centre in South Africa, where he has been a senior faculty member for over 15 years and delivers a module on "Coaching in the African Context" or "The Wisdom of Africa in Coaching". He is also a part-time faculty member of the Business School at the University of Stellenbosch, teaching a module for the MPhil in Management Coaching on "Ubuntu Team Coaching".

Dumi is an author on executive coaching, Ubuntu intelligence (UbuQ), Ubuntu coaching approaches, and human connection. He is a regularly featured speaker and panellist on topics relating to coaching, leadership, and people development. Dumi also recently featured as one of the speakers in a TEDx event convened by the University of South Africa (2021), talking about human connection through "conscious, mindful and intentional" greetings.

Dumi lives in Johannesburg, South Africa, and works globally.

Editor's Foreword

In this book, Dumi Magadlela has presented us with a gift, one for which I have waited a long time.

As we move further into the twenty-first century and away from the COVID-19 pandemic, we are also leaving behind the concept of tight command and control in the workplace, replacing it with more emotional intelligence, inspirational and human-based leadership to bring out the competence, intelligence, skills, and potential of those we lead and manage. It is becoming more evident that everyone in the workplace has a role to play in terms of leading, managing, innovating, creating, building culture and fostering relationships that acknowledge the more humane and collective aspects of our working together.

Dumi introduces us to the essentials of management with an Ubuntu underpinning, including the importance of conscious greeting, understanding, and building a collective sensibility, and becoming less selfish and more aware of others and how they experience us. This also resonates with the need to develop a willingness to engage differently in a world which requires greater human connection amidst the complexity of our social and economic circumstances.

Ubuntu management and coaching can help us in building a new team around an identified purpose. It becomes more important when the task requires skills, perspectives and approaches, such as the ones found in the wisdom of Ubuntu that helps shape transformational human relationships. Ubuntu is an ancient worldview, way of being and way of life, which can be explained literally to mean *I am because we are*. It can be described as a *"way of being"* as much as an African philosophy. Ubuntu is embodied practice which shows up best in interrelationships, as it is inherently relational.

In his book, Dumi shares the value of Ubuntu for leaders and managers struggling to build humanity-based and high-performance teams. He presents the powerful concept of Ubuntu coaching as it is used in "onboarding" (introducing and coaching new leaders into their roles as leader-managers). The philosophy of Ubuntu that Dumi encourages us to adopt is possibly what can most help us to better engage with our common human values – and to more effectively negotiate our differences, tensions, and conflicts widely across organisational cultures.

One of the takeaways from this book is the focus on how Ubuntu management and coaching can be used to effectively socialise and induct new employees. This is a key to building the kind of *team* that will help the new leader-manager to make a significant mark quickly, laying foundations for deeper long-term impact and a positive legacy. In the wake of artificial intelligence and related digital technologies being introduced across increasingly virtual and hybrid workplaces, genuine human connection will only become more vital, especially for leader-managers.

Sunny Stout-Rostron DProf
Series Editor: Management Mastery and Practice Series

Acknowledgements

It has been a rollercoaster ride of learning and self-discovery, and especially self-awareness, for me to work on this little book with the masterful Sunny Stout-Rostron. Not only is Sunny a prolific writer and brilliant editor, but she has also been incredibly patient with me while putting this small project together. I am eternally grateful for your amazing writing mentorship, Sunny. I look forward to writing more, and better!

To my team and home crew, thank you Mosa, Sandile, Nobuntu and Lwazi Magadlela for letting me live in the study while researching and writing this. You inspire me to do and become more of me every day. To all members of the Magadlela clan around the world, keep shining. There is so much to explore and become in this rather short human lifespan. Tell your stories loudly and boldly.

I am humbled to take this opportunity to thank my former long-term employer, the Development Bank of Southern Africa (DBSA), for the amazing opportunities to serve across beautiful Africa, and gain exposure to countless engagements to coach, lead, and facilitate training sessions and all manner of client contact sessions that have supported my growth. I am richer and wiser now from my 17 years of service in the DBSA.

Thank you to my onboarding, leadership, teams, and coaching clients around the world who have enabled my continuous learning – including my coaching home, The Coaching Centre with Dr Paddy Pampallis, where I have grown as a coach practitioner. That is where I first met Sunny, in our module on Integral Practitioner Coach training.

And finally, thank you Knowres Publishing for this opportunity to put my thoughts and voice out into our fragmented and connection-hungry world.

Dumi Magadlela PhD

Glossary of terms

Conscious connection: The ability and capacity to safely engage with others without fear of attack or rejection. This refers to the creation or co-creation of an environment or atmosphere where every individual or group within a specific setting (for example, in an organisation or workplace), feels seen, heard, and recognised as they are, and thus are connected and free to check in, inquire after, and relate to anyone else in the shared space without fear of intimidation of any kind. It is an environment where everyone sees others as they are, and as they present themselves. Connection is achieved when people in shared spaces feel that they can freely express themselves and showcase their skills, talents, natural or learned abilities and gifts without hindrance, to the benefit of the group, team, or organisational system in which they collectively serve.

Emotional intelligence: As defined by Goleman[1] and Goleman, Boyatzis and McKee,[2, 3] this is about how leader-managers handle or navigate their emotions and relationships. It is about the ability and capacity to identify our own and others' emotions correctly, and then be able to manage relationships better. When we are clear on what these emotions are, we can manage them appropriately as the situation requires, and for the benefit of everyone involved. Emotional intelligence is a skill that can be learned at any stage in a leader's life. Mastering emotional intelligence can be a superpower for new leader-managers in times of transition and rapid change.

Employee socialisation: Enrolment and onboarding of new employees in their jobs in a way that enables them to become operationally functional and to play a significant and positive role in their team and the organisational system.

Heart-set: This refers to a "state-of-heart" as distinct from a "state-of-mind" or mind-set. It is about one's heart, feelings, intuition, and emotional attunement. It involves being aware of – and alert to – where one's strong feelings are positioned and emanate from, and what they are anchored on. It can literally be about what one's heart is set on. Reference here is made to the importance of shifting from a cognitive centre (the head) as our guide, towards the chest and mid-section of the body. The idea is to become more integrated, and not mainly head-centred. It is about all "sets" and "centres" working together in a more integrated way – the head, heart, gut, and hands all working in unison towards agreed goals. It is "this *and* ...", and not "either-or".

Intempathy: This refers to *live and intense empathy* in practice and action. It is the act or practice of consciously and intensely focusing on sensing what another person is feeling, and then acting on it to support them in the moment (as opposed to *sterile empathy* of words or empty gestures with no action to help another). It involves seeking to feel how a fellow human being feels in the moment, and what to do to assuage pain or suffering. Intempathy is consciously going beyond stepping into another person's shoes. It involves *stepping into their heart-sets*, their feelings, their sensitivities in the moment. It also involves being *intensely attuned* to a fellow being as they process and/or deal with something that affects them intensely and requires the support and emotional availability of others in the moment. Timing is essential in intempathy; it is not something that can be postponed or put off until a more convenient time later. Unlike hyper-empathy or what has been termed "over-empathy" or "toxic empathy", intempathy is both positive and other-centred. It is based on or informed by Ubuntu values, and is part of the spirit of living with and exhibiting Ubuntu intelligence (UbuQ) qualities. I have often called it Ubuntu mindfulness in action; it makes better sense that way.

Lekgotla: This word in the SeSotho or SeTswana languages of southern Africa means "meeting place". The *lekgotla* is a meeting place or space, or "time-in-a-place" as allocated for the team or community to meet and safely discuss any issues that need input. It is equivalent to the safe space described by Nancy Kline as the Thinking Environment®.[4] In a traditional *lekgotla* setting across southern Africa, everyone in the gathering is afforded the same respect and opportunity to express their views and be listened to and heard. The leader *consciously invites* everyone's voice into the gathering. This *lekgotla* is imbued with psychological safety; in fact, psychological safety comes standard as a given in a proper *lekgotla* setting. This could be the team's regular meetings or other scheduled team sessions where everyone can freely and safely show up as they are. In my languages, isiZulu and isiNdebele, this sacred meeting space is called *inkundla* or *idale*.

Onboarding: Like socialisation, this is the process of fully engaging and capacitating new hires to become effective role-players in their functions, and to understand how things are done in their team or teams, their department or division, and in the rest of the organisation. They get to learn about the culture of their new environment, and to understand what normal practices are and what is not acceptable.

Social Intelligence: This is more than being "street smart". I prefer to refer to social intelligence as having "social smarts", a bit more socially savvy than just being "street smart". It is the ability to successfully navigate and/or manage social interactions and social relationships in different contexts without negative manipulation or use of force, power, rank, status or other forms of authority. This may differ from, or build on, the definition given by Daniel Goleman in his book *Social Intelligence*.[5]

Team: A team is a relatively small number of people who consciously choose to work together towards achieving a common purpose or a clearly defined goal, objective, or task. There are multiple types of team in the fast-changing world of work. Increasingly now there are virtual teams comprising people in different geographical locations who are able to collaborate or team up to deliver on a shared purpose or on specific tasks. Teams can be engaged for short-, medium- or long-term initiatives, and are always changing. Sometimes a team may be dissolved after the achievement of its goal, task or purpose.

Team coaching: This refers to the process of working with a team to help it achieve defined targets, goals and purposes. Great team coaching supports a team to amplify its holistic worth for itself, its stakeholders, the whole organisation, and its partners. Team coaching involves contracting with the team leader, with every team member, with the whole team, and with the system within which the team exists. It also involves engaging with the team on a regular basis, and can be one of the most powerful ways for a new leader-manager to build or grow their team and make a significant impact within a relatively short space of time.

Ubuntu: This means humaneness and being aware that we are inextricably interconnected. It means that I can become fully human only when I recognise the humanity of fellow humans too (*I am because we are*). It also means that I am who I am because you can become who you define yourself as, or who you wish to be. In other words, we are all integral parts of one interconnected human ecosystem. Our shared vision must be to help each other become the best versions of ourselves; and not just some of us, but every single one of us. Together we can be whatever we desire to be, and thus achieve incredible feats that we could only dream of if some of us take part while others are excluded. With Ubuntu as the common *way of being*, humanity is far greater than the sum of its (often intentionally divided and unconsciously separated) parts.

Ubuntu coaching: This is coaching using Ubuntu lenses, practices, principles, values and humaneness. Ubuntu coaching is about seeing and feeling the humanity and greatness of others as part of the coach's interconnected social and human ecosystem. Ubuntu coaching is coaching using humane grounded-ness and deep conscious presence, that starts with "seeing" the client or the team as an extension of the self or the coach. Ubuntu coaching is inherently systemic in conceptualisation and in practice.

Ubuntu intelligence (UbuQ): This is about living daily with and practising Ubuntu, humaneness and genuine connection with others and intentionally or consciously seeking to connect and build mutually enriching and positive relationships. Ubuntu intelligence is the ability to navigate social relationships in ways that benefit those involved in the relationships without conscious or unconscious prejudice or discrimination. Ubuntu intelligence requires new mind-sets and especially new *heart-sets* that enable us to see the self in the other, and most importantly, to feel genuine empathy and connection with other beings. Ubuntu intelligence equips us with "laser eyes" to see through the layers of taught narratives about others, to see them as they present themselves in shared safe spaces. Neuroscientists have discovered that as humans we are born with this inherent connection to others, and then we learn and are carefully programmed to separate and to become "other". Ubuntu intelligence removes the layers, and frees us from the learned separating and programming, and from our smaller circles which are often laced with (sometimes unconsciously) taught biases and stereotypes.

Chapter 1

Introduction

The aim of this book

This book provides tips, guidelines, exercises, tools and coaching suggestions for new employees joining teams in leadership or management roles. It presents and explores behaviours and practices for onboarding and ensuring effective functioning of new leader-managers with a particular interest in supporting and promoting human connection and engagement in shared spaces. The book presents ideas on how best leader-managers can build their new teams, especially in fast-changing and unpredictable work environments. It helps new leader-managers co-create and build high-performance teams from the outset.

It is a book about how to engender genuine human interconnectedness, and offers ways to *consciously connect* with people in mutually enriching relationships. It touches on the context of our fast-changing and increasingly *virtual* and hybrid world of work that can be likened to the Wild West of nineteenth-century America. The book shares carefully selected tips for onboarding new leaders in the digital world, and in contexts where social media ensures that information is shared far and fast among employees who may not even be within the same time-zones.

The starting point of the book is a leader-manager's entry into an existing organisational system through recruitment. As the new hire joins an existing formation, and depending on the role they play in it, they may need to build their own team or group, and often within a short period of time. The starting point could also be establishing a new team and supporting that group to become operationally effective. In any case, the group concerned is what is referred to as the leader-manager's "new team" in the book.

The book's focus is therefore leader-managers who want to build dynamic, high-performing, value-creating teams. This requires skilful human interrelationship skills, which are not assisted by technical expertise or positional authority alone. This book, and the series in which it is published, offer the much-needed tools to navigate the new normal. While *human connection* is at the heart of the book, the attributes, behaviours and practices of new leader-managers that help shape their immediate impact are also explored. The selected tips and practices featured in the book are meant to assist leader-managers in building powerful networks of groups, teams, or communities of belonging within their organisations.

You will notice that in this book I use both the terms "leadership" and "management" freely with reference to the team leaders who are either joining existing teams or establishing new teams from scratch. The reason is that I am including all leaders, managers, team leaders, supervisors and other professionals with responsibility for supporting a group, team or other collective in efforts to achieve specified shared objectives.

Reference to leadership and management is not in the strict, conventional definitions of the two concepts. It is aimed at covering all areas of leading others, without narrowing this down to either leadership or management in their common definitions. It seems to be generally accepted that leadership and management may be different. For example, Rukuni clearly differentiates between management and leadership when he argues that:

> managers plan, budget, manage staff, solve day-to-day problems, build and maintain systems and procedures ... in aid of controlling the organisation and achieving greater predictability in results and outcomes. Leaders ... establish direction, establish strategy, align people, motivate and inspire managers.[6]

Sunny Stout-Rostron has coined the term "leader-manager" in her first book in this series:[7]

> We are working with becoming a leader-manager – mastering both leadership and management skills to 'achieve results through others' (the classic definition of management). We need to talk about both leadership and management if you are to be successful in inspiring, motivating, upskilling, and stimulating the highest potential and performance from your team.

> Leader-managers need agility, the ability to learn, and the ways and means to manage conflict. At the same time, they need to develop resilience, emotional intelligence and empathy among their direct reports and team members. They need to be functionally savvy, with an ability to learn fast and go deep with their people to help them discover who they are and how they can achieve their potential.

Every well-meaning organisation needs an effective employee socialisation and onboarding process that helps new leader-managers in their efforts to build new teams. Some leader-managers are better able to enrol and socialise themselves into their new spaces and in their new roles than others.

This book focuses on onboarding practices as a means to ensure that the new leader-manager has a broader and a comparatively fuller view of their new landscape in the organisation. This is meant to provide them with a deeper understanding of the range of possibilities available to them to build their new team as quickly and effectively as possible. We look at different scenarios during and beyond the crucial processes of socialising or onboarding new employees and leader-managers into their new roles in organisations. The challenge is to raise the bar for the new hire to see their new organisational terrain and people landscape as an opportunity to co-create something new and special.

The book goes beyond onboarding, induction and orientation as a human resources (HR) process for getting new employees familiar with how the business or organisation runs. It also focuses on the process of igniting or garnering human connection in shared spaces, on leader-managers and/or team leaders taking charge of processes, groups, teams or other social configurations that seek to collaborate to achieve agreed-upon objectives.

The focus of this book is therefore not only on the process of socialising new hires prescribed by line management and/or the human capital or human resources function. It is also about what I prefer to call the "nuances of human engagement". These are the human connection practices that are not in the onboarding manuals, but are nevertheless critical to initiating genuine connection. "*Conscious greeting*" is one of them, and this is outlined in Chapter 6.

The multifaceted ways in which a new leader-manager sets out to build relationships with their new team and the broader organisation therefore comprise a major focus of this book. How do new employees or new team members really connect with their colleagues? What is the social or team "glue" that binds them together to be able to collaborate and *become* a value-adding team?

My view is that it is the *vibe* created among team members that is a catalyst to good relationships. It is that feeling, sensing and connection that lights up the spaces between and among humans. This is the essence of any relationship. As coaches, especially with Gestalt influences, we know that sometimes we must coach the relationship between the client and their system. (Gestalt is a systems-based psychological school that believes in working with the energy of the system as it emerges and is presented.)

Another position on this subject is that while the formal induction processes and new employee orientation programmes are taking place, there are other, more nuanced enrolment processes happening with the new employee or leader-manager. These may be even more crucial than the prescribed formal processes.

The book focuses on Ubuntu as a less tested but potentially powerful perspective and instrument for building a diverse, dynamic and potentially high-value-creating team within organisations. It is a universal phenomenon and not a preserve of a few so-called enlightened individuals or groups in advanced cultural contexts, imagined or real.

Using Ubuntu values, principles and lenses in employee socialisation and onboarding or in building a new team helps to empower new leader-managers to show up more confidently. It also actively enables organisations and their management teams to "see" each new hire as the much-needed asset that they were seeking. Granted, the organisation may have set out to acquire this new leader-manager asset in order to help improve a part of the business that they identified as needing the asset's skills in the first place.

Ubuntu tools, tips, strategies and frameworks will help the new leader-manager to lay solid foundations towards building their new team. Hence the book uses and deploys Ubuntu in the field of coaching and employee socialisation as an essential ingredient in enhancing human connection. Ubuntu coaching is a catalyst for connection in an increasingly fragmented digital world and organisational new normal.

The approach of this book

The book presents a selection of tips and strategies for new leaders, managers and team leaders joining organisational systems and teams, especially in fast-changing times. It is a quick and easy read for new leader-managers who want to build their teams and develop their new or desired high-performance and value-adding cultures.

Sections of this book are meant to challenge established patterns and practices of human connection. They are also intended to suggest and present alternative ways of connecting that may not necessarily work in every scenario or context. These new or alternative ways may require some getting used to. For example, "conscious greeting" in Chapter 6 may not be familiar to many people. Yet it may be just what the situation requires for genuine and authentic connection to be established, especially during the first weeks or months of a new leader-manager in a team or organisational system.

This book features relatively limited theoretical foundations, focusing mainly on Ubuntu, with a few carefully selected interview-based case illustrations, anecdotes and short stories. There are practical exercises at the end of every chapter, with tips on how to handle everyday challenges of connection as a new leader. Most importantly, the book is meant to assist leader-managers to avoid the pitfalls that can cause them and their teams to struggle in their connections and engagement roles and responsibilities.

This book will not drown you, dear reader, in spreadsheets, tables, lists of data and graphs, or in statistic-after-statistic of what percentages of new hires leave after how long in their new jobs. Nor does this relatively short book present detailed tables and graphics on what conditions will make organisations benefit fully from the qualities of a new arrival in a significant role.

What the book covers instead are carefully selected practices, stories, key strategies, mind-sets, and especially what I call *"heart-sets"* that are needed by the new hire, their new team, and by the human capital or human resources team for them to excel. Parts of this book can also be used by line management, especially to help support and position the recruit to settle into their role. The book recognises the value of all key stakeholders in helping a new leader-manager settle in and start delivering or performing. The new leader-manager will be well-placed and empowered to lead their new team after reading this book.

The roots of this book

Among my major influences over the years has been my upbringing in a rugged rural setting where I learned to live off the land and livestock. To this day, gardening is one of my favourite pastimes and among my most preferred *mindfulness* practices. Having studied the social sciences, including the sociology of human behaviour, alongside social and cultural anthropology, I grew to love observing people. I gradually became ever-curious about human interrelationships and human development. Individual leadership coaching and team coaching have been natural steps on my journey in people development. While I have enjoyed and been fascinated by every part of it so far, there is clearly still a lot more for me to learn about people and human development. These connection practices help me stay curious and linger longer on the learning edge.

I first encountered Integral thinking during my doctoral research in the 1990s. Then in 2007, I received a full immersion in Integral theory at one of the premium coach training schools in Africa, The Coaching Centre in Cape Town, where I enrolled for an Integral Coaching Diploma. The school was founded and is led by Dr Paddy Pampallis, who is a pioneer in Integral thinking infused with African wisdom in the development of professional coaches. (Incidentally, the first facilitator on the coach training programme was the editor of this series, Dr Sunny Stout-Rostron.) Over the years, I have grown to appreciate the multifaceted nature of human connection, and the various lenses we use to look at, perceive and try to understand our complex worlds of human coexistence.

Integral theory and thinking, as popularised by Ken Wilber and several others, provide a useful working map for navigating our shared world. This theoretical base offers powerful handles for working with systems-based frameworks, approaches and philosophies (ways of being). It also relates to, and complements, theoretical frameworks such as Ubuntu and Gestalt psychology as applied in organisations. An Integral future infused with *valuing* every voice, every gift and every part of our shared humanity can support the emergence of a "new way of being". This works even better within organisational systems which place genuine and authentic connection in the centre of relationships within and across all shared spaces. The starting point for this Integral reality is our inevitably diversified, increasingly interconnected, and yet fundamentally fragmented virtual world of work in this new digital normal.

Wilber, Patten, Leonard and Morelli[8] and other Integral "believers" position Integral theory as a framework for organising not only ways of thinking, but also life and practice in an unpredictable and constantly changing world. One quotation that captures some of my own thinking about life, work, coaching, and especially our shared ways of being, is the following: "An Integral framework can help you make sense of the many options available to you, providing ultimate flexibility and inclusiveness, so you can most fully and deeply honour your intentions and fulfil your potentials".[9]

Over time, my own thinking and practice from my upbringing, and my coaching practice and human relationship management, have all been influenced by reading and working with these relatively new Integral maps. I have generally tended to spread my approaches and working tools across a range of theoretical and philosophical foundations. Experience shows that with human beings, there is no one-size-fits-all.

Integral theory is only one of the lenses and tools I have gathered over the years and use to navigate my coaching engagements. As a transformational coach with Ubuntu, emotional intelligence and systems thinking, I have included multiple tools in my ever-expanding coaching toolbox. I have also included in this book some of the coaching models that I have developed and applied in my practice over time. Other tools include emotional intelligence, Gestalt International Organisational Systems Development, various assessment tools (including the Enneagram and Discovery Insights), and Ubuntu coaching.

Ubuntu coaching is one of the core approaches to genuine human connection at the centre of this book. Most of my life has been influenced deeply and profoundly by Ubuntu principles and the inculcation of the Ubuntu way of being, which ensures that we value the views, voices and full presence and engagement of others and the greater collective in everything we do. In other words, I learned early to bring others into just about anything that has greater collective value or worth beyond the individual.

My Ubuntu coaching framework is not only deeply experiential for me, but it has also been powerfully influenced by the work of fellow Ubuntu coaches and Ubuntu consciousness practitioners over the years. My understanding of Ubuntu coaching was broadened and deepened after taking a course for practitioners in March 2021 called "Ubuntu Coaching for Coaches", designed and delivered by Nobantu Mpotulo, an ICF-accredited Master Certified Coach. This course shared Ubuntu-informed engagement tools and practices that have been seen to deepen profound human connection throughout the coaching engagement from the first encounter.

In the Ubuntu way of life, the individual serves the collective, the community, or the shared and inspirational greater good. Every individual in an Ubuntu-led society understands that they have a responsibility to their fellow beings, and are therefore accountable for their wellbeing and the wellbeing of everyone else in equal measure. Individuals do not place themselves above others or serve themselves to the detriment of others. The "inclusiveness" mentioned by Wilber et al.[10] in the above quote speaks to the Ubuntu spirit of "seeing" and valuing everyone else and the collective good above individual interest. I have gotten used to calling this dance between Ubuntu and the Integral framework the *"Ubuntu Integral stance"*.

A significant part of this thinking has been shared by and with Dr Paddy Pampallis through her Integral coach training school mentioned above, and her consulting business the Integral Africa Institute. A significant part of the development of my Integral lenses can be attributed to my work with the Integral Africa Institute and The Coaching Centre for over 15 years. Dr Pampallis, who has been a great friend and colleague, shared the following lingering question about navigating our shared coexistence: "How do we navigate this all to create a society where difference is valued, where sameness and integration is not a grey amorphous mix of non-commitment and unexamined assumptions?".[11]

Navigating the multifaceted differences that characterise our world requires tapping into hitherto unexamined narratives about ourselves and others, and experiencing the unfamiliar. It requires us all to challenge our existing or dominant assumptions not only about others, but also about ourselves, and what we believe to be true.

In 2006–2007, I was fortunate enough to be part of the seventh cohort on the Gestalt International Organisational Systems Development Programme (Gestalt-IOSD) of the Gestalt Institute of Cleveland in Ohio, USA. I learned how to work closely and deeply with change and transformation in organisational systems. It helped me to see the systems and their levels in organisations far more sharply than I had done before.

During my leadership skills development journey with the Institute's Gestalt IOSD programme, I had the privilege of learning from Jonno Hanafin, who was one of our teachers and facilitators. It was during this time that Hanafin shared insights about being an *"awareness agent"* at any level of every system that we work with or in.[12] This is one phrase that best describes what I do in my journey as a one-to-one coach, as a team coach, or a gestalt practitioner within organisational systems. Coaches help develop awareness; hence I regard us coaches as awareness agents.

One additional root of the human connection thoughts and reflections shared in this book is the power of the village in which I grew up, where I was taught to greet every "stranger" I met just about everywhere. This was inculcated into everyone in such a manner that greeting became the norm. Similar villages exist across most of sub-Saharan Africa, and in other formerly colonised parts of the world. The message is that there are no strangers really; just friends and acquaintances we have not yet encountered. I have carried this in my heart wherever I go, and it directly informs some of my thoughts and reflections in this book.

Who is this book for?

This book is for all people who start out in new teams, organisational systems or other shared spaces involving interpersonal relationships, and seek to make an impact. It is for everyone who wants to share their vision, plan, or strategy towards achieving shared goals, and requires the participation and collaboration of others to deliver it. It can be used by managers and leaders in corporates, non-profit organisations and multilateral institutions. It can also be used by non-managerial professionals who want to build teams and inspire them towards the achievement of their shared goals. It is not only for business coaches supporting leader-managers joining new teams, or human capital professionals and other workplace people-development practitioners.

I hope that our coaching peers and fellow leadership skills development practitioners, along with human resource professionals, will find some useful nuggets in the following pages to use in their own inexorably changing practices.

How to use this book

The best way to access the many tips, suggestions and recommendations in this book is to take it in small bite-sized chunks, and per relevant chapter or section. Another way is to keep it light-hearted and not take things, or yourself, too seriously. There is a light touch to the style used in writing the book, and it is meant to be less academic and more accessible to a wide range of readers including leader-managers, life and business coaches, HR practitioners, and consultants in the field of leadership and management development.

The idea was always to keep the content less theoretical, and less heavy or dense, with as little academic abstraction and philosophising as possible. There is nothing wrong with theories and philosophies; sometimes they give us useful handles and help explain complex phenomena. But this book is closer to being a toolkit with user-friendly tips than it is to being a textbook for reference purposes.

Chapter breakdown

Chapter 2 introduces the concept of teams in the overall context and environment of fast-paced change, the emergence of the virtual world of work with its different characteristics, and new elements such as the hybrid workplace and a VUCA (volatile, uncertain, complex, ambiguous) or BANI (brittle, anxious, nonlinear, incomprehensible) environment.

Chapter 3 discusses employee onboarding and socialisation techniques and methods for igniting human connection towards building your new team. The concluding section in the chapter shares anecdotal messages from a selection of clients and leader-managers making recommendations and giving useful tips for entering new organisational systems.

Chapter 4 reviews some models and frameworks for the onboarding and socialisation of new recruits. There is a focus on what works best in transitional contexts, especially for new leader-managers joining their teams in the new normal.

Chapter 5 explores the ever-important subject of emotional intelligence, and how these skills provide useful and powerful tools and tips for authentic human connection. Managing and running successful and effective team meetings, especially as a new leader-manager, is also addressed.

Chapter 6 introduces the concept of Ubuntu coaching as a catalyst for developing genuine and authentic human connection as new leader-managers are brought on board to existing teams. The Ubuntu coaching concept and practices, alongside Ubuntu values and principles, are shared here as a potentially powerful resource and foundation for growing solid connections across teams. This chapter also introduces the new concept of Ubuntu intelligence, alongside the other new term of intempathy (intense empathy), as tools for managing change and transition during socialisation of new leader-managers. It presents one of my favourite subjects, that of greeting others consciously. Consciously greeting others assists with igniting genuine and authentic human engagements that support human connections that build strong relationships.

Chapter 7 features interviews with three highly skilled and experienced business coaches adept at using Ubuntu concepts in their practices. In *Chapter 8* the book takes the reader and the new leader-manager within themselves, with a set of seven Self-Reflection Questions to help deepen the leader's self-awareness. The questions also help sharpen the leader-manager's understanding of what they need to adjust or tweak in their new leader-manager role, to land with impact in the team.

Chapter 9 concludes, bringing the book's messages together by highlighting – one more time – the role and value of establishing genuine human connection from the outset, especially as an incoming leader-manager. It reiterates several of the key takeaways from the book, and ends with an invitation to seek to engage and connect across any and every level of any system where humans require connecting and collaborating.

Chapter 2

Teams at work

Teams have clearly defined goals, values and targets towards which they are working. They have their own unique cultures and attributes, and are heavily dependent on inherent human connection. Without their shared purpose, they are just groups of people convening for expediency, with little else in common. Teams also focus on growing members' resonance around shared interests and beyond superficial boundaries of roles and levels within their collectives, or as defined by their organisations.

A VUCA or BANI world

If it is anything, the twenty-first-century workplace or organisation is unpredictable. A large part of the unpredictability is a direct result of innovative technologies, the Fourth Industrial Revolution, and fast-paced changes in the constantly globalising business environment. The context of this book is our increasingly virtual, digital and hybrid world of work, featuring organisational systems and other shared spaces that seem to be in constant and unpredictable transition.

The acronym "VUCA" became synonymous with the fast-paced changes associated with the Fourth Industrial Revolution and innovative mobile technologies after it was coined by economists Warren Bennis and Burton Nanus in 1985. It was popularised by the US military, which used it to describe the new and uncertain global geopolitical situation after the collapse of the Soviet Union in the early 1990s.[13]

Penteado describes the terms of the acronym in a clear and unambiguous way that I find useful in working with organisational groups and teams:[14]

- *Volatile:* The environment demands that you react quickly to ongoing changes that are unpredictable and out of your control.

- *Uncertain:* The environment requires you to take action without certainty.

- *Complex:* The environment is dynamic, with many interdependencies.

- *Ambiguous:* The environment is unfamiliar and outside your expertise.

The above descriptors of the VUCA terms have stayed with me since I read them. I have continued to use them in some of my team coaching, onboarding and team-building support to clients and their teams in organisations.

As already mentioned, the advent of mobile technologies and social media and the general explosion of communication tools has seen many teams and organisations remain tuned-in to work even during so-called after-hours. Technology, and the growing work-from-home phenomenon, has seen managers, leaders and teams stay connected to each other and to work platforms wherever they find themselves at all times, presenting mixed challenges amid unprecedented opportunities of connectivity and constant availability to others.

One rather strange coincidence is that the term VUCA sounds exactly like the word *vuka* in my language isiZulu, which literally means "Wake up!" This conjures up images of military training camps when new recruits are being woken up at dawn to start training. It also evokes memories from my boarding school days when the house master would wake us all up early with shouts of *"Vuka! Vuka mfana!"* (Wake up! Wake up, boy!) to get us ready for school.

In the new world of work, it is the responsibility of every leader to ensure that their teams are up and ready to take on the challenges of a fast-changing environment characterised by volatility, unpredictability, complexity and ambiguity. New leaders owe it to themselves, their teams and their organisations to wake up, stay awake, and remain alert to sudden changes, twists and turns in their environments. In the context of a newly-recruited manager or leader, especially one who is intent on building their new team to become whatever they desire, it is crucial for them to *vuka* (wake up), and be alert to the language, rituals, practices, norms, values and informal structures of the group. Getting to know this upfront, or at least early on, positions the new "chief-to-be" well towards gaining a deeper understanding of their new team.

In this VUCA environment, leadership is an especially challenging undertaking. Anyone seeking to actively lead anyone else, a team or an organisation, must brace themselves for serious and unrelenting constant examination. The former CEO of Microsoft, Satya Nadella, eloquently summed up this leadership conundrum:

> The role of leadership today is to bring clarity in uncertain times. The more uncertain things are, the more leadership is required. There is no job description for what you are facing, no rule book … today's leaders need to thrive in the face of this uncertainty (quoted in Penteado).[15]

Ironically, it has been suggested that the term VUCA is itself now obsolete due to the increased speed of change experienced as a result of momentous technological disruption, political upheavals, and global crises such as the COVID-19 pandemic and climate change. Influential American futurist Jamais Cascio has argued that conditions are no longer uncertain, they're chaotic and completely unpredictable; while what happens is no longer simply ambiguous, it's incomprehensible.[16] Accordingly, Cascio created an updated framework for working with chaotic futures, BANI, the terms of the acronym having the following meanings:

- *Brittle*: The situation is easy to shatter, and systems and organisations are prone to sudden and total failure, because they are subject to catastrophe at any time. The COVID-19 pandemic showed that the world is highly fragile, and many businesses are fragile with it.

- *Anxious*: There is fear that any choice we make might be the wrong one. Due to the VUCA world, there are now so many uncertainties that people generally feel immense anxiety over what could go wrong regardless of the actions they take.

- *Nonlinear*: Increasing disconnection between cause and effect have made what was formerly complex now seem nonlinear, or without a single meaning or structure. Events seem disconnected and disproportionate, so a small decision might have devastating consequences, and it appears no longer possible to have structured organisations.

- *Incomprehensible*: Situations are extremely difficult (if not impossible) to understand, and attempts to find answers no longer make much sense. Rather than simply making role-players resigned to chaos, however, considering a situation undecipherable may be what is needed to motivate them to step forward and find their own path.[17]

Sridharan suggests the following approach to coping with the challenges posed by a BANI world:[18]

- If the situation is brittle, develop capacity and resilience. Strengthen teams by improving collaboration, investing in training, and adopting distributed structures. Always prepare an alternative, even for systems that are apparently working well.

- Counteract anxiety with empathy and mindfulness. Dealing with employee anxiety requires empathy from the company, which can be strengthened by training staff to develop their emotional intelligence and interpersonal skills. Increased situational awareness is also required, because only if a team is aware of a situation can they control it, and only if they can control it can they manage it.

- A nonlinear situation requires adaptability; it should be approached with no expectation, but rather with fresh eyes and a candid, open attitude. In such circumstances, rigid plans will be a burden on business, and companies which don't innovate but rely on proven methods will not be able to adapt quickly enough.

- Something that is incomprehensible requires transparency and intuition, because organisations will not be able to wait to fully explore what is happening before making decisions. Misunderstandings can be avoided through the use of technologies such as artificial intelligence, big data and data science.

Introducing FACE

My take on VUCA and BANI is that they assume a slightly negative angle on how humanity is dealing with the challenges we are facing. My stance on emerging realities is to be a little more positive, rather than merely underlining the real limitations imposed by the volatility, uncertainty, complexity, ambiguity, brittleness, anxiety, nonlinearity and incomprehensibility of fast-paced changes.

To this end, I came up with a new acronym, almost tongue-in-cheek, that I believe best describes and defines our current technology-fuelled changes, especially in the wake of – and explosion of – artificial intelligence and the virtual, hybrid and complex world of human relationships. I have called this FACE, and not just because reality is in our faces daily; more so because we are unlearning and re-learning how to confront or face our common and collective challenges as fellow humans.

FACE can be broken down as follows:

- *Fast*: The technology being introduced in workplaces and across all levels of society is fast, and reaches far-flung places almost instantly. Leader-managers can recruit, train and engage their teams in remote places with unprecedented speed and efficiency.

- *Available*: Besides the limited and limiting digital inequality in some poorer corners of the world where internet connectivity is unreliable at best, large parts of our global village are now inextricably interconnected via the internet and other easily accessible tools and applications. And some of it is getting cheaper. With artificial intelligence tools such as ChatGPT and Bard, this promises to increase availability and access to more information and knowledge that leader-managers can use to connect and grow their teams globally.

- *Connected*: Newly available technological tools such as artificial intelligence support leader-managers to become aware of their impact and reach across their new teams. These connecting technologies are assisting in growing humanity's awareness of the impact of climate change across vast geographies. All this points towards increasing systemic awareness across the globe, especially among younger people, and the need to connect across superficial differences such as race, gender, or divisive dichotomies of "developed" and "developing" or "under-developed". Within organisational systems, leader-managers are learning that being connected with every member of the team, and not using rank, helps create resonance across their new teams regardless of the distances between or among them. Better yet, using the lenses of Ubuntu when working with these new technologies enhances connection and deepens any team's capacity to influence bigger systems faster.

- *Enabling*: Successful leaders are inherently enablers. Some of the largest companies globally since the 1990s have been in the business of enabling and equipping humans to do better and faster whatever it is they seek to do. Leader-managers with impact are essentially enablers of greater team efficiencies and effectiveness through co-creation, which thrives in an enabling environment.

Effective teams and teaming in the new normal

The workplace as we knew it, as we think we still know it, is likely to be transformed forever into something with which we are not yet familiar. Even this very message is getting old.

While some employees enjoyed working from home during the COVID-19 pandemic lockdown, some expressed deep feelings of guilt when they had to step out to pick up essentials, even for a short time. Others expressed concern about their family situations when they had to go back to the office. Yet others were frustrated with managers who did not feel their staff could be trusted to work from home. (That "T" word again, trust. This is a rare commodity. If you find it in your team or organisation, protect and preserve it, invest in more of it, and nurture it with everything you have.)

Post-pandemic, there were mixed feelings, indicating that there is likely to be an urgent need for at least two major interventions, as follows:

- Employee wellness support in regard to psychological (mental and emotional) health.

- How to galvanise teams and help employees re-enter and become productive team members.

It will therefore be important for employees to have capable psychologists, therapists, counsellors and certified coaches ready to jump in and support their team to navigate this transition into the unknown.

Further, however, as we transition towards the largely unknown "next normal", one area of workplace dynamics that is likely to have a major impact on workplace productivity is teamwork. But what are teams, and what should organisational leaders and managers know about teams and teaming? My generic definition of a team in an organisation is a collection of individuals around a shared purpose that they feel can best be achieved through cooperation, collaboration, and mutual accountability over a given period. In essence, I regard a team as a group of people working together towards a shared collective goal. A team has a common membership, characterised by interdependence on each other, and guided by mutual respect.

In transformed and positively dynamic workplaces, a good team is characterised by a group of people working towards a shared goal, and they all know that they matter. Yes, in a team, all members' contributions matter. Team members are able to speak freely about what is working and what is not working. They are also able to hold each other accountable to one another, to the team and to the organisation they collectively serve. In sports like football, a good team is characterised by team members who instinctively know where their teammates are, and what the best move is for the team to achieve the desired result (score a goal, and not an own goal!). They aim to win together.

The work we all have in our teams is to determine whether we really are a team, then work towards getting better at it. The connection flows from the teaming effort. The Global Team Coaching Institute (GTCI) defines "teaming" as "a process over time, both within and between teams, of commissioning, clarifying, co-creating, connecting and collectively learning".[19]

The most effective teams in the next normal will be those that do not concern themselves too much with ego and hierarchy. Characteristics of such teams will define their teaming. These attributes will include creating what in coaching we call "psychological safety". This is a way of interacting in which all members of the team not only feel free to make positive contributions, but do not fear having their heads "chopped-off" when they share an idea which differs from or contradicts their team leader or manager. The next normal team member and leader is almost ego-less, and works selflessly for the greater good of the team and the organisation.

Psychological safety is the belief that you won't be punished or humiliated for speaking up with ideas, questions, concerns, or mistakes. And it is a *shared belief held by members of a team that others on the team will not embarrass, reject or punish you for speaking up*. When you have psychological safety in the workplace, people feel comfortable being themselves. They bring their full selves to work, and feel OK laying all of themselves on the line.

In his book *Smarter Faster Better*, Charles Duhigg explains five core components needed to create alignment in teams:[20]

- Teams need to believe that their work is important.

- Teams need to feel their work is personally meaningful.

- Teams need clear goals and defined roles.

- Team members need to know they can depend on one another.

- But, most importantly, teams need psychological safety. To create psychological safety, team leaders needed to model the right behaviours.

Exercise: Psychological safety in your team

Complete the following statements:

1. Three things that my team, people around me, and my direct reports fear about me are: …

2. The three things I consciously do to develop or grow psychological safety in my team are: …

3. Three things in my team or direct reports that make me uncomfortable or feel unsafe are: …

4. Three things about my team or direct reports that make me feel safe and able to thrive are: …

Great leaders know that every single human being has greatness within them – regardless of gender, race, age and other factors. Effective organisational leaders recognise that one of their most important tasks is to ignite the greatness that resides within each employee and enable everyone to express themselves fully – without fear of retribution or ridicule. Creating safety for everyone to be fully themselves is one of the most critical roles of a leader. Effective teams that add value to their organisational systems have safety and accountability built into them.

For a team leader to say to themselves that they are the best leadership development instrument they have or could ever wish for, results from practical experience of leading effectively. To lead effectively, team leaders must fix their *how*, especially how they show up in every encounter with members of their team and all their stakeholders.

Who people consider themselves to be shapes how they show up. Team leaders who know this are better positioned to seek to improve themselves. So, who the leader is influences their leadership style, and how they impact the team they lead. This means that the person the leader is within themselves, including the leader's mood in any moment, has a direct effect on the people they lead. This in turn has a direct effect on the climate or atmosphere that the leader co-creates in the shared spaces and with their team members, regardless of the formal structure of the organisational system.

This could be stretched to mean that the leader's "vibe" indirectly influences the kinds of result the team achieves together. Leaders who know that the team is a system nested within other, larger, systems, understand that everything and everyone is inherently interconnected. New members coming into their teams are thus regarded as new energy fractals that help freshen and strengthen the team and the organisational system, and must be embraced and welcomed as assets.

Not all leaders and managers in charge of teams *really* fully understand the latest research, thinking and best practices in team management. And that is OK. These things can be learned. That is what management consultants are for. And management coaches can help leaders and managers to clarify, define and prioritise just what they need to learn.

So, what is your best team attribute? Make sure it includes having everyone's back. Can you work well with others and feel "part of" something bigger than you at all times? Or do you prefer the solo run? The cliché is spot-on: there is no "I" in team. Team up.

One of the most salient features of the new normal in organisations is the increasing reliance on technologies that provide on-demand data and information for leader-managers about their performance or the performance of their team members. Similarly, a critical skill that new leader-managers can develop, grow, refine and sharpen on an ongoing basis is listening. In a fragmented and disconnected world of work, where people are sometimes treated like automatons or machines on a production line, listening is increasingly important, especially for leader-managers seeking to build new teams. Effective listening requires creating time to sit together with team members and build good enough rapport to be able to inquire about their lives. This is why conscious greeting is an integral instrument in the toolkit of the new leader-manager.

Conclusion

As a new leader-manager, building an effective team is one of the most critical tasks. This is likely to be an ongoing process that does not end when the new leader-manager is confirmed in the role. Great leaders of teams are constantly contracting and re-contracting with their teams to ensure that they keep their finger on the pulse and energy dynamics of the team. Effective teaming means that the leader-manager must get to know each team member well enough to support their growth and development. This requires most of what this chapter has covered in elements of team coaching that enable and empower both the new leader-manager and their team.

Chapter 3

Onboarding and socialisation

My adventures in onboarding

In my 30 years of work experience, one of the most challenging yet exciting roles I performed was as Regional Manager in a public entity. The programme I worked in was tasked with recruiting senior engineers, financial experts and planners, and deploying them in low-capacity municipalities across South Africa. Most local governments in this country have chronic skills shortages that are crippling their capacity to serve their communities. They have only a limited number of skilled or experienced professionals capable of performing the urgent tasks of helping government deliver on its development objectives.

I learned a great deal about working with local government officials in socialising new members into this sphere of government. In South Africa, municipalities represent the delivery arm or service delivery level of government, intended to provide desperately needed public services to citizens. I had over 50 people in my region, covering three provinces. As the Regional Manager, my team comprised a diverse mix of male, female, old, young, local and international professionals with varying levels of skill across various disciplines including engineering (mainly civil), finance and planning. I was aware that they came into the team with different motivations. Some were desperate for work just to have income to feed their families and pay their bills. Others were retired and at the end of their careers, yet still seeking to get into roles where they could keep busy while continuing to serve and mentor those around them.

Since my team was spread out across three provinces in South Africa, I regularly visited them in their stations. I got to see and hear what socialisation challenges they encountered on the ground. Many of them were retired from roles as senior professionals, and had previously been living in large cities such as Johannesburg and Cape Town. Some of them came from neighbouring or regional states such as Zambia, Zimbabwe, Namibia and Botswana. They were mainly experienced seniors with scarce skills who were being brought back to fill in areas that desperately lacked their skills. I can clearly recall meeting some of them and de-briefing, socialising and onboarding them into their new roles as part of our induction processes.

One of my lingering memories in this phase of introductions of new team members into my team concerns the issues they raised during our discussions. While the purpose of my meeting with them was to support their settling in and orientation into their roles in the programme, I quickly learned that a significant proportion of their clarification issues and questions upon arrival – and soon after deployment – involved who they would be working with in their deployment stations. They were also intensely curious about whether they would be able to build effective working relationships, especially as they were largely from outside the specific areas in which they were to be deployed. Establishing effective relationships, or building their new teams, was a key concern for many of these senior professionals.

The ever-willing and supportive HR and administration teams always made sure that they provided all the working tools, materials and notes the new recruits needed to start their work and be operationally active in their new roles. What the recruits needed most was a clear picture regarding the lay of the team-building landscape that they were going to be joining. In my visits to where they were stationed, one of the leading subjects of discussion was how difficult it was to build relationships and be trusted by their fellow employees within the municipality. The lessons gained from these engagements about human connection, or lack thereof, will stay with me for years to come.

As an executive coach using Ubuntu coaching and Ubuntu lenses, I have worked with diverse organisational leaders and teams across different sectors around the world. I have also had opportunities to implement formal induction, employee socialisation and onboarding processes for new employees. My journey has also involved planning and implementing induction and orientation programmes and employee engagement sessions for many professionals. Part of my experience in designing and implementing organisational culture change journeys or programmes has led me to believe that at some deeper level, human beings want to belong to a group.

A key lesson from my experience has been that the first few days, weeks or possibly months in a new employee's entry into a team or organisational system feature a select few crucial determinants of whether or not they will stay long in the system. Their entry, and how they are received, can make or break their career early on. Furthermore, the early engagements they have can provide clear indications of what kind of impact they will have in the business. I am not suggesting that the first days, weeks or months of a new employee's tenure can help provide a clear prediction of their future success. I am suggesting that this period can yield some indications.

Granted, human behaviour is not an exact science. In late 2020 I enjoyed a few months' stint as the Acting Head of Learning and Development in one of the leading financial services organisations in South Africa. This gave me an opportunity to understand some of the leading ideas and insights into how human capital or human resources teams work. I was especially interested in how human resources teams conduct the process of employee induction, onboarding and socialisation in the short to medium term. One of the first lessons I learned was that this is not as easy a role as it may appear on paper; it requires a lot of patience and understanding, and meticulous attention to detail. Accordingly, my respect for HR professionals across the board was greatly enhanced.

Over time, I have noticed that some organisational leaders do not give due credence to the importance of socialising new employees into the culture of the organisation. Some organisations tend to leave it all to their HR teams, and in the hands of HR business partners. That is not enough. The process of new employees' socialisation is everyone's business.

The importance of onboarding

I believe that first impressions matter. I do not believe that they are everything where new recruits within organisations are concerned. First impressions may be everything to some leaders or managers, but not to everyone, and not all the time, and especially not in the same way. Yet they still matter. A lot.

Onboarding new employees into their new roles within organisations is one of the strategic responsibilities of the human capital or human resources department. There are multiple reasons why organisations must do more to make onboarding and accompanying processes work better. One of the biggest challenges, and a critical business case for deploying more resources to ensure effective onboarding, is the potentially crippling risk of new hires leaving soon after they start work, with the organisation thereby losing great talent before it can contribute or make any significant impact in their new roles.

The virtual world of work requires even greater attention than the in-person context to support new employees' enrolment into their new teams, departments, or the rest of the organisation. A common theme among organisations hiring millennials and other young people is that they can be unpredictable and hard to please. For many new employees, especially younger ones, the first few days, weeks and months in a new job are crucial in determining whether they will stay longer in their new role or pack up and leave in search of a new, and possibly more welcoming, work environment.

When first appointed, many managers and executives have a mix of excitement, exhilaration and a level of being terrified or at least anxious about the new role. It is normal to feel some anxiety and a rush of adrenalin when starting a major assignment. The crucial stance is to stay alert and become increasingly aware of the organisational language spoken and not spoken to you as a new hire. In this regard, as a newly recruited leader, it is to your advantage to quickly become aware of all the signals, crucial information and intelligence around your new role. Hence the value of *conscious onboarding*.

For seasoned managers and leaders who have led groups or teams in large or small organisations, the process of building a dynamic team can become a personal mission to leave a legacy. It can also become a nightmare that leaves open wounds, scars, or social and psychological debris that the team, the leader or the organisation would rather do without.

Onboarding needs careful thinking-through and planning to be implemented successfully. How a team leader, manager or even a company board executive gets introduced (or introduces themselves) to their new team can sometimes make or break their impact in that team. In many cases, it may determine how soon new employees can start making a positive impact either as a team member or as a leader.

What is onboarding?

Onboarding or employee socialisation is the process of introducing a new team member, a manager, a leader or another role-player, into an existing or a new team. One common definition of onboarding is that it is:

> the process of helping a new employee to fit in with your organisation. That includes welcoming them to the team and making them feel part of the company culture. It also involves getting them up to speed with tools they'll need to do their job.[21]

Often, onboarding or employee socialisation is not differentiated from induction and staff orientation. These related activities are all part of the much-needed processes that support the introduction of new employees to their workplaces and the teams with which they will be working. They are interrelated activities that describe the often unappreciated and critical process of a new employee's organisational socialisation. This book does not dwell on the differences among these related or similar processes, but rather emphasises the value to be placed in carefully co-creating your desired team, together with the team members themselves. For creating a well-functioning team is not the sole mandate of the team leader – it the responsibility of all team members. Hence the use of the term "co-creation".

In his book *Onboarding*, Charles du Toit (2019) differentiates between three types of onboarding: psychological, functional and cultural. More specifically, Du Toit describes these three different areas as crucial dimensions where real onboarding takes place.[22]

Psychological onboarding

Du Toit (2019: 2) refers to onboarding psychologically as helping a new hire or fresh recruit to become "a functioning member of the team". In my view, this requires a generous helping of the "psychological safety" discussed in the previous chapter, in which the members of a team or group feel free enough and safe enough to fully express themselves without fear of retribution.

New leaders and managers who can help co-create such an atmosphere in their first few months of joining the team are more likely to succeed than those who evoke fear or come across as intimidating. As Du Toit suggests, to onboard an employee psychologically results in the full socialisation of the new hire and helps deliver a "functioning member of the team".[23]

Employee socialisation or onboarding works better when the team leader starts from a clear intention to "build the new team" towards high performance or excellence. This requires that the new leader or manager works towards co-creating a collective atmosphere filled with honesty, transparency and open engagement. Managers and leaders who tune in to their teams' emotions are more likely to achieve resonance with their teams than those who are rigid and work only within structures and levels. Those who seek others out are the ones who practise "meeting others where they are", and do not focus mainly on their positional authority.

This is different from leaders who constantly push, bully and threaten others to join their team. Leaders and managers who create positive and vibrant teams are not obsessed with their location on the organogram. Those who rely on the structure for their authority tend to inadvertently create toxic environments where performance temporarily peaks during the hype or fear of repercussions by the bully-leader, and may then flatten or dip soon afterwards. Resonance born out of genuine connection is more likely to ignite the creativity of the team and raise performance in a sustainable way, than are fear and threats of retribution.

A high-performance organisational team grows easier and flourishes in an environment where the members know that they can be themselves and speak up honestly without negative repercussions. They also know that when they openly criticise or challenge their seniors, there will be no negative consequences. They truly feel safe. There is psychological safety in the team. This scenario of safety is a typical *lekgotla* atmosphere or environment as described by De Liefde,[24] and similar to Nancy Kline's Thinking Environment.[25] De Liefde positions this clearly when he argues that:

The pillars of tribal leadership – humanity, dignity, trust, respect, sharing and entrepreneurship are universal. These values apply throughout the world … they are not the preserve of tribes in … [indigenous communities] but can prove their usefulness in every cultural context. The starting point is that the tribal leader acts in accordance with the pure intention of serving the community. In this way, the manager [or leader] empowers others to develop and improve their qualities.[26]

It is the responsibility of the manager or leader of the team to help shape the environment in which the team operates. But successful development of this enabling environment for the team depends inherently on a collective effort.

Exercise: Building trust within the team

In order for team members to feel safe with each other, it is important to build "trust" within the team and between each member of the team, by having all team members answer the following questions together:

1. What behaviours are preventing us from collaborating and building deeper trust with each other?

2. What assumptions are we making about each other that cause us to behave inappropriately?

3. What needs to shift within each of us in order to have a more mature response to these assumptions?

4. What positive, appropriate behaviours should we use to build more trust with each other?

Functional onboarding

The second dimension of onboarding that Du Toit refers to after onboarding psychologically is "onboarding functionally".[27] He describes this dimension as involving the process of helping the new employee become functional in their role. This would be demonstrated by them "doing the job which they were recruited to do at the standard that is expected" in that specific position.[28]

Besides the anxieties associated with starting a new role in a new organisation, it can be an intimidating situation for a new team member to come in and start to lead effectively. To be functionally effective requires that the new employee ticks all the performance boxes quickly enough to avoid being perceived as either ineffective or invisible.

Many organisations, especially through their human capital teams, invest substantial amounts of time and resources towards onboarding their new employees to ensure that the new hires become quickly familiar with the organisation's operational systems and processes. The sooner new employees understand the details of how the business functions, and the quicker they start delivering on what they were employed for, the better for everyone. Hence the power – and often understated value – of the delicate process of onboarding.

Cultural onboarding or socialisation

The third dimension that Du Toit highlights relates to one of my favourite focuses, and this is onboarding culturally.[29] Du Toit argues that this is about ensuring that the new team member is "aligned to the company culture and values".[30] I recall studying social and cultural anthropology in my graduate studies, and one thing that stuck with me was the notion that all cultures serve a specific purpose and gradually shift, evolve and change as and when new situations require adjustment.

Organisations, like countries, have their own cultures and sub-cultures. Organisational culture can be the glue that keeps everything together in a team. Culture can also be the fuel that gets people and teams – and organisations – fired up and delivering on their team goals and targets. A well-known organisational culture definition is that it is *the way we do things around here*. The work of the new hire is to figure out what that is rather quickly. The new employee will do well to quickly be aware of, and work with, the existing culture or ways the team or group operates. Where the new hire is the leader or manager of the existing team or group, the responsibility to help build rapport and connect to the rest of the team becomes even more important.

Regarding the culture aspect mentioned by Du Toit,[31] Philippe Rosinski[32] says that "A group's culture is the set of unique characteristics that distinguishes its members from another group." While onboarding is taking place, for however long it takes – and it can be a drawn-out socialisation journey – part of the work of the new recruit is to scope out and become fully aware of and familiar with the way the group does things. In this regard, there are formal and informal processes of engagement with the new team or group. I cannot emphasise enough how important it is for the new manager or leader who is joining an existing team to quickly learn the "engagement language" of the team. This includes learning and fully understanding all the numerous signals that team members send to each other; and there could be a lot of them.

Onboarding therefore includes a process of enrolling a new person into your existing culture. If culture is the way we do things around here, onboarding is about helping others familiarise with, and be operationally effective in, that specific culture. One could therefore describe onboarding as the *process of enculturation* that an organisation puts its new employees through in order for them to become functional and operational in their new roles. Great onboarding or socialisation is more than an opportunity for marketing and branding the business to the new hire. If you want to be harsh, you could say it is cloning a new and better employee than the existing or previous one.

The process of onboarding new employees into their new roles can be regarded as a potentially powerful and game-changing injection of fresh energy and thrust towards delivering on what they were hired for. As an organisational behavioural scientist and professional coach myself, I can clearly see why some of us coaches sometimes refer to onboarding as the *socialisation* of new employees into the culture, traditions, norms, values and ways of functioning effectively in an organisation.

The way new employees experience their new workplace indirectly speaks to the culture of the organisation. A welcoming organisational culture starts engaging the new hire before their start date. This is often called "pre-boarding". It is among the crucial elements recommended to create those vital positive first impressions in the psyche of the new hire.

Ideally, successful employee socialisation helps the organisation shape the views of the new employee to become an asset for the business into the future. Successful onboarding, therefore, is a crucial period for checking whether the new hire is a good fit for the desired or aspirational organisational culture. The socialisation experience for the new employee must be such that the new hire effectively becomes a passionate ambassador for the business and organisation. It all starts with effective connection.

Beyond onboarding and socialisation

When onboarding is done well, there is little chance of new employees wondering why they signed up. They are inspired to serve in their new role. Their behaviours demonstrate keen interest in understanding the team's dynamics. Great new leaders quickly understand where they need to focus, engage or intervene in order to facilitate greater group or team awareness.

In this book, I use the phrase *employee socialisation* alongside "onboarding", not just because I am a social or behavioural scientist by academic background. I believe that this better explains the interrelated processes and concepts of getting new leader-managers and new employees to be fully enrolled into their new functions.

The initial enrolment processes of employee onboarding or socialisation is absolutely crucial. But building your new team goes a step beyond that phase. It is about inspiring others, and igniting genuine human relationships resulting in solid connections and rapport, which establishes groups or teams with clear goals, purpose, vision and membership. It is also about rallying yourself as a leader or manager to serve fully and selflessly in any role within a team. This essentially requires that as a leader, you enrol others in your vision, values and purpose, and bring them on board towards what you want to build and eventually leave behind as part of your legacy.

While the rest of the employee onboarding and socialisation processes unfold as per written HR policies or organisational guidelines, there is a finer process of both formal and informal relationship-building engagements taking place. These are what we can call *"extra-boarding"* interactions. They are explored here as part of – and going beyond – the well-known processes of old-school, structured onboarding. This does not negate the role and effectiveness of the prescribed employee socialisation engagements. It is about finding what works best where, when and how.

A team is built not only on formalities such as those in induction, orientation and/or employee initiation into the *"business of the business"*. While these are crucial, they are not the only essentials in building a team as a new recruit. Genuine and authentic connection with a new team, especially as an incoming member or leader-manager, is among the best foundations from which a new hire should start off.

In some contexts, new hires may seek to mark their territory by somehow "putting everyone in their place" for them to know "who is boss". There are new managers and leaders, or bosses, who immediately seek to ensure that everyone submits to their new-found positional authority. The scenario of animals marking their territory remains not far from the mark for some new managers and leaders. The discussion of "conscious greeting" in Chapter 6 includes some recommendations and tips for gaining influence without unnecessary domination, or without the need to impose yourself on the new team as a new leader.

Human beings and their organisational systems have often been referred to as ecosystems. We have seen countless examples where leaders who "feed" on the energy of their people eventually suck the life out of their teams, resulting in dysfunction or the system breaking down. It is like the proverbial dictator who wants to rule everyone with an iron hand.

Reuel Khoza starts his book *Attuned Leadership: African humanism as compass* with a powerful statement that has stayed with me: "Leaders are not just born to the role. They are born, then made – and sometimes unmade by their own actions. A leader who is not in tune with the followership will become a leader in limbo".[33] What Khoza is referring to here is the stance that the leader or manager needs to take as they position themselves in relation to those they lead or to their whole team and/or organisational system.

Being in tune with the followers early on ensures the establishment of early rapport and connection. This sets up the new leader or manager for success in efforts to build their new team. Lack of attunement, or being out of tune with the followers, builds resentment and discord, and may result in disconnection between the leader and their followers.

New leaders with self-confidence and a clear understanding of their roles and tasks can be deliberate in how fast they start making their mark in their team. Once appointed, new managers know that they will sooner or later make their mark on their team. They know that it does not matter how long it takes for them to be effective.

Powerful new managers and leaders tend to want to always be in good control of their intended impact. Few manage to remain in control without imposing themselves on their new team. Early in their tenure, new leaders are capable of carving out a route to the hearts of their new team with some specific activities that often garner support for new tasks or inspire support while igniting great rapport with the new "chief".

Nussbaum, Palsule and Mkhize,[34] in their book *Personal Growth African Style,* discuss the power of making a good impression. They refer to the work of Gafni[35] on leaving "soul prints" on everyone with whom we come into contact. Gafni emphasises that our soul prints are our spiritual signatures, and that when we encounter others, and interact with them, we "imprint" our souls on them in more or less the same manner we leave fingerprints on the surfaces we touch with our hands and fingers.[36]

Creating a Team Agreement

In one of the first meetings with your team, you will want to establish the appropriate behaviours for the team when discussion and decisions are easy, as well as when tensions arise. The exercise below helps establish a Team Agreement that becomes the start of your team charter. The purpose of this exercise is to create connectedness between team members, and to help them, at the beginning of their journey, to decide on appropriate behaviours necessary to create a shared way of being together.

An example of the cultural norms and behaviours defined by one team recently is provided below the exercise.

Exercise: Creating our Team Agreement

Break the team into smaller groups and have them answer the following questions – each group writing up their outcomes on flip charts.

1. What behaviours do we expect from the entire team in the way that we work together?

2. How should we act and respond to each other if and when things become difficult between us?

The groups then come back together, and in a plenary session combine the behaviours into a final list that becomes the Team Agreement. Members of the team will hold each other to this Team Agreement in order to be able to do their work together; the behaviours defined in the Agreement become the team's cultural norms. It is important to be sure these behaviours align with and underpin the organisation's values, and so they must each include a verb.

Once the Team Agreement has been finalised, go round the whole group, with each person in turn sharing their personal commitment to the team by answering this question:

3. What will be your personal commitment as a team member to this leadership team and to your functional team, going forward?

When team members answer the above question, remember that each person should speak once before anyone speaks twice.

Example of a Team Agreement – our cultural norms

This is an example of a Team Agreement that Sunny Stout-Rostron recently helped a corporate team create as a way forward in a difficult environment.

A. What behaviours do we expect from the entire team in the way we work together?

1. Affirm each other.
2. Be supportive.
3. Listen and be attentive.

4. Encourage different perspectives.

5. *Respect* – be respectful:

    - Celebrate wins, big and small.

    - Be vulnerable.

    - Consider people's point of view – don't dismiss them.

    - Hear everyone.

    - No late-coming.

    - No devices in meetings – and listen.

    - No distractions – and focus.

6. *Clarity*:

    - Listen, and don't speak over people.

    - Put yourselves in their shoes, in the shoes of the audience.

    - Content should be relevant.

7. *Respond*:

    - Hear people, listen and understand.

    - Hear other points of view.

    - Ask more questions.

    - Do not be defensive.

    - Be open.

    - Consider others' frames of reference.

B. How should we act and respond to each other if and when things become difficult between us?

1. Be respectful.

2. Don't be personal, deal with the issue.

3. Sleep on it.

4. Do it face-to-face.

5. Be there for each other.

6. Check-in on each other.

7. Don't weaponise a setback.

8. An injury to one is an injury to all.

9. Don't be dismissive of other viewpoints.

10. Be willing to be influenced by another point of view.

11. Set boundaries.

12. Be succinct and clear.

13. Be decisive.

14. Respect decisions made.

Leadership in the new normal

In his book *Shaping the Future of the Fourth Industrial Revolution*, the founder and executive chairman of the World Economic Forum, Dr Klaus Schwab, argues that "We can use the Fourth Industrial Revolution to lift humanity into a new collective and moral consciousness based on a shared sense of destiny".[37] This is a noble stance for rich nations to have. The Fourth Industrial Revolution has ushered in major innovations which have resulted in life-changing technological and telecommunications connections bringing significant advantages to hitherto disconnected and often neglected parts of our shared humanity.

However, evidence from decades – if not centuries – of global commercial dealings does not lend hope to the likelihood of genuinely working together towards lifting humanity into "a new collective and moral consciousness" as Schwab implores.

At the end of his book, Schwab presents a compelling case for collaboration, arguing that:

> The scale, complexity and urgency of the challenges facing the world today call for leadership and action that are both responsive and responsible. With the right experimentation in the spirit of systems leadership by values-driven individuals across all sectors, we have the chance to shape a future where the most powerful technologies contribute to more inclusive, fair and prosperous communities.[38]

The scale and complexity that Schwab describes, and the scope or extent of the challenges currently experienced, are constantly expanding and appear to be at global scale.[39] What remains short or missing are effective tools which establish, enhance and deepen genuine connection when diverse people, from all walks of life, meet each other. There seems to be skewed representation in multilateral entities such as the very World Economic Forum Schwab founded, and the United

Nations Security Council. These international bodies need to heed calls such as that of Schwab.[40]

This starts with the recognition of our inherent interconnectedness, which is located in "connection literacy". Connection literacy involves "seeing" others as they are, and not judging and/or placing others in boxes or categories based on one or other criterion they had no role in defining. The same principles operating at international multilateral levels are at play at organisational systemic and human interrelationship levels.

Workplace challenges of globalisation have seen an explosion of virtual, hybrid and matrixed teams in workplaces. This has made it critically important for leaders to have human connection tools and practices with the capacity to assist them in establishing strong and meaningful relationships. It all starts with conscious engagement and conscious greeting.

In the fast-changing world of work (the new normal), there is a delicate connection touch required from every digital-age leader and manager appointed to lead others. One of the critical elements of this new environment is that access to information is no longer as much a source of power as it was before. Now, employees have access to a great deal more information than the leader may be aware of. Leaders who still believe that access to information can be directly associated with power and control are living in an indefensible delusional state. The best stance for newly hired employees who join teams and organisations in transition is to be a curious learner first, and the appointed leader or manager later.

As discussed in Chapter 2, our world of work is now a VUCA (*volatile, uncertain, complex, ambiguous*) or BANI (*brittle, anxious, nonlinear, incomprehensible*) environment. Accordingly, I suggest the following tips for building your new team in these challenging conditions:

- *Volatile*: Stay in tune with, and connected to, all your team members and at all times, to have access to what they know and to be available.

- *Uncertain*: If you are new and trying to build your new team, you do not necessarily have a to know everything. Work with what you have.

- *Complex*: Complexity is your friend when you want to build your new team. Embrace it, and model ways to live and work with it. Show confidence.

- *Ambiguous*: The unfamiliarity of the environment is similar to uncertainty, and demands that as a new hire building your new team you handle different and strange scenarios well.

- *Brittle*: Strengthen the resilience of your team to systemic shocks by improving collaboration, and ensuring that there are always backup plans in case things go wrong.

- *Anxious*: Reduce anxiety by staying focused and engaged, showing empathy to team members, and keeping them briefed to maintain awareness of relevant business situations.

- *Nonlinear*: Promote adaptability by keeping plans and systems flexible, encouraging team members to maintain an open outlook and to suggest improvements where necessary.

- *Incomprehensible*: Maintain transparency, and strengthen the intuitive understanding of team members through briefings, training, and the use of appropriate technologies to promote rapid comprehension of changing situations.

An onboarding and socialisation dialogue with a marketing magician

Below is a partial transcript of an interview with Ms Makho, a senior marketing professional in a leading South African ICT corporation based in Johannesburg.

Q: What are team-building practices that you recommend for dynamic new chiefs?

A: One of the great practices is that as a new employee I need to be assured that I did not make a mistake by joining the new employer, and I get this from my initial encounters and behaviours exhibited by my new fellow employees. To me it is simple, and it is this: make me feel good that I made the right choice. Do nothing that will make me freak out and regret joining the new business.

Q: Where does the process start for you to feel well-socialised?

A: It is simple for me. The induction or orientation must be assuring and affirming of my big decision. It's like a marriage or personal relationship to me – I must feel that you care as a business, otherwise I'm out. If you see in the early days that your new partner is abusive, or potentially (and evidently) a sociopath or a psychopath, give me one good reason why you would choose to stay with them? And if you stay, who do you have to blame if down the line you suffer from the very signs you saw early on? Organisations tell people who they are and how they treat their people. Believe them first time during induction and later during the whole onboarding process.

Q: You mentioned having a warm culture that makes you feel welcome. Where does this start?

A: Easy one, that. If as a new employee I walk through the company premises and meet people who do not bother to say hello, let alone make eye contact, to me that is a red light. If as a business you did not have the decency to have someone wait for me or at least receive me upon my arrival, then I know I will be up against some major culture obstacles. I start to brace myself for a cold organisational culture, and that simply gets my back up, and you can be sure my defences are on alert for a hostile atmosphere. New employees must feel welcomed. Greet everyone you are not familiar with. We are supposed to be members of the same family after all, right?

Q: Thoughts on rolling out the red carpet for senior employees and not bothering with the rest?

A: In my view, there must be no difference in welcoming any new employee. The organisational structure is often only partially correct when it comes to real leadership anyway. We all know at least one executive or senior manager who was an absolute jerk. I could use stronger words, trust me. And we know of junior employees with incredible leadership capabilities who just need a break and an opportunity to showcase their skills. Sometimes hierarchical structures are mere obstacles, and these are reinforced by narrow-minded onboarding processes that see power residing in positional authority. Embrace everyone as a new asset, and you may unearth serious gems of talent.

Q: How would you like to see new employees socialised into new workplaces during the first few days?

A: On a lighter note, I would give them all each a clearly visible name tag that says 'I'm new, tell me why I should stay!' [Laughter.] But seriously, great companies make new employees visible and celebrate their arrival. I don't mean a luminous yellow vest or large, orange, cone-shaped hat. Just a visible badge at least for a few days. I am not one for an intimidating initiation process like some people do in boarding school, in some sports teams, or in the military. That is bullying, and it must be illegal. The idea must to engage with new recruits and ask them questions about themselves, and be genuinely interested in knowing more about them and their career aspirations.

Q: So, you do believe in conducting some kind of welcoming rituals?

A: Yes, some welcoming rituals are OK. They must be smooth and well-considered, though. As a newbie, do not make me feel like I am being interviewed all over again. I am done with that. Keep it within my new team and/or department, and make sure that it is clearly meant for me to learn and for my new colleagues to know more about me. For example, limit it to my first meeting with my new team. After a few weeks, I like it when my new employer convenes a meeting to welcome me and other newbies in a broader setting and asks us all to share something that we like or do not like about our new work environment, our new teams, and the rest of the climate.[41]

This conversation with Ms Makho led to new insights about employee onboarding. One of the lingering reflections and insights was the value of genuine connection from the outset. The insights from Ms Makho were enhanced by her emphasis on the importance of avoiding engagements that appear to be "teaching" the new hire in condescending ways, and avoiding the feeling of interrogation as if the new employee were being interviewed all over again. This happens especially where there is little genuine connection. There is a premium prize in creating psychological safety for all new employees to feel at home in the new system.

Welcome aboard, Lerato – let *me* show you around

This short story is based on true events, with the names changed, and is aimed at illustrating and demonstrating the existence of multiple onboarding interests that affect a new leader-manager coming into an already well-established system.

When Noma, the head of the Training Academy in a small consulting company, retired, it took five months for her replacement to be appointed. Every part of the business supported by the Academy was ecstatic when the new leader, Lerato, joined the business. Everyone was lining up to show her around.

In the company's organisational structure, the Training Academy was located within the Corporate Services Department. One of the leaders in the Department, Nicole, who happened to be at the same management level as Lerato, took it upon herself to spend hours daily with Lerato showing her around and teaching her about the business.

What later emerged, however, is that this "showing around" was really about "onboarding" Lerato to Nicole's faction within internal departmental politics, in order to have more leaders on Nicole's side. She was not onboarding Lerato for Lerato's sake, nor was she doing it to help prepare Lerato for her new role and job in the Academy. Rather, Nicole was "feeding" Lerato only one side of many multifaceted stories.

The highlight of the "informal onboarding" by Nicole comprised the negative perceptions and opinions that she shared with Lerato about certain members of the team Lerato was inheriting. Nicole painted three of them as lazy, incompetent, and not to be trusted with urgent or important tasks. The mistake Lerato made, especially after a few lunches and dinners with Nicole, was to swallow whole everything Nicole told her, and then start treating these three team members as if they were incompetent. It later emerged that Nicole's request for an expensive executive leadership training course at Harvard Business School in the USA had not been approved during the interim period, and she blamed these three Academy team members for that.

After her probation ended and she was confirmed on the job, Lerato worked with an external coach and started to build new relationships with her team members. She also hired several new team members to run the Academy with a full complement of staff. It took over a year for Lerato and her team to build good working relationships.

Among the lessons from this quick anecdote are the following:

- Formal onboarding must be structured and carefully managed by a responsible party.

- Informal onboarding can be damaging for the team and leader-manager if left unchecked.

- New leader-managers must prioritise creating psychological safety in their new team.

- Factional games in the organisational system must not be allowed to affect formal onboarding.

- Sometimes it helps for new leader-managers to give their team members a fair chance to present themselves to the new leader and tell their own stories about their strengths and gaps.

Conclusion

This chapter shared insights into the new world of work and the requisite connection tools, practices and skills leaders need to build resonant and well-functioning relationships with their teams and others in their diverse networks. The new world of work demands new ways of engagement and new human relationships. In efforts to overcome barriers to new relationships, including challenges posed by workplace dynamics such as virtual and hybrid teams, leaders are using new virtual tools and practices which ensure they can both "see", "reach" and "touch" their teams from wherever they are around the world. Technological changes call for new and hitherto untested ways of engagement. New leaders need to engage fully with their new team members, agreeing behavioural norms and creating deeper connections from the start. The interview with Ms Makho demonstrated the need for new ways of connecting with new employees. This requires that organisational leaders need to unlearn old ways and learn new ways to connect with their new team members.

Chapter 4

Onboarding and socialisation models

"When the root is deep, there is no reason to fear the wind" – *African proverb.*

This chapter introduces employee onboarding and socialisation models which enhance genuine human connection within organisational settings. The chapter starts by presenting Du Toit's six-stage model of employee socialisation.[42] This is followed by the introduction of an onboarding model called RAMGARD.

The six-stage model of employee socialisation

Du Toit[43] describes onboarding as a longer-term process than induction, and one that has the following six stages:

Stage 1 – *Alignment*: Who is going to do what, and why?

Stage 2 – *Land the fish*: The period between the new start signing up and their first day on the job.

Stage 3 – *The first days*: When the new start arrives at work for the first time.

Stage 4 – *Getting to know the company.*

Stage 5 – *Getting to know the department.*

Stage 6 – *Getting to know the job*: Getting to grips with the specific role for which they are responsible.[44]

This six-stage model is useful to track how a new recruit is doing on the journey towards settling into their role. The model could be enhanced by first describing the context that sets up a conducive environment for the new hire to settle into their role, even before establishing the "alignment" in Stage 1. In my view, another missing piece is a detailed description of the nuances of the socialisation process that actively helps the new employee to feel genuinely on board and functioning effectively as a team player. This goes beyond what the employee functionally does in their new role to help themselves get on board. It includes what the existing team does together with the line manager to help the new hire settle in. This is about initiating the development of enabling and empowering relationships for both employee and employer.

RAMGARD: Introducing a connection model for employee socialisation

One of the models I have used in my coaching practice supporting new hires is called RAMGARD. I came up with it after tracking several journeys of new senior employees across different sectors, roles and levels in their organisations. I decided to name it RAMGARD based on the steps clearly visible – it is really the broad steps or stages of the process that matter most.

The RAMGARD Model is drawn from actual experience with coaching clients and observation of their journey as the onboarding process unfolds and they endeavour to build their new team, or in many cases, as they seek to first understand and then either join their new team or change it. The reader will note that this varies in application depending on organisational context. What remains useful is the broader journey a new employee goes through as they seek to settle in and then start building their new team.

The RAMGARD Model to build your new team consists of the following steps:

1. *Recruitment* process at the start.

2. *Arrival* and first impressions during the first few days.

3. *Meeting*, greeting, connecting with and *seeing* your new team.

4. *Growing* your signature, team identity or brand.

5. *Adjusting* your new team colours.

6. *Reviewing*, strengthen your strengths, and test for take-off.

7. *Developing* new leaders to lead the team in the future.

A walk through the stages of the RAMGARD Model

This section provides a more detailed description of the different stages of the RAMGARD Model, as applied to different scenarios or situations. The deployment of the Model is always contextual, and there is no one-size-fits-all application that suits all situations.

The RAMGARD Model was designed as a guide for onboarding any new employees who want to make an impact in the organisational system they just joined. It is helpful especially for those in leadership or management roles who are working towards building their new team.

1. Recruitment

The first stage in building your new team occurs during the *Recruitment* process. The new team leader-to-be must choose carefully whether this is a suitable system to join, fitting their vision of themselves and their career. There will be early signs indicating whether this is the right place, chief among them being the connection they feel to the place through the team that runs the recruitment. Do you feel listened to, heard, noticed, or do you feel like just another number to tick on the recruitment list? Are you dealing only with the HR team, or do you get to connect and engage with line management even before the recruitment process is finalised? What does it *feel* like going through this recruitment process? This process often ends with the signing of the offer letter. In some cases, it continues through probation.

2. Arrival

Arrival on the job, even virtually, is part of *acceptance* of becoming part of the new team (even when this has not fully formed yet!). Sometimes *Acceptance* is used instead of *Arrival* in the Model to signify the choice the new hire is making before full enrolment and socialisation into the new role. Rituals such as the signing of the employment contract, and being taken through the induction, orientation and initiation processes, are part of arrival. *Arrival* may also include visits to different parts of the organisation (scoping and familiarisation with the terrain or territory covered by the team). This stage of the model emphasises the new recruit's entry into the system.

3. Meeting

The third stage in the RAMGARD Model involves *Meeting*, greeting, connecting with and clearly seeing your new team. This may be virtual or in-person. In either case, the new recruit starts to see, speak to and connect with their new team members. This is the start of the crucial process of building rapport and laying foundations for solid relationships later. The message I have shared with my clients here is that every encounter with anyone in the team involves literally a sensing of whether they can trust you, can work with you, and can be open and vulnerable with you.

Where the team is going through major changes or the previous incumbent (manager or team leader) has left, the onus is on the new leader to find out quickly how to navigate the rugged relationship terrain. It cannot be a continuation of the same, or a worsening of the situation. This is one reason why Drucker,[45] in writing about how to manage ourselves, said "We have to place ourselves where we can make the greatest contribution to our organisation and communities." We choose where to place ourselves or be placed, and it must be a conscious decision with choice backed up by intent. I want to join this team and this organisation because I believe that I will be able to make a difference and make part of my life contributions whilst I am here. Most crucially, the new employee at this stage of RAMGARD is saying that these are the people with whom I will be doing this. Meeting them means seeing them as they are, and not as I have been told they are, or been made to believe they are.

Ideally, when you join a new team, it is best to let them tell you – and then show you – who they really are. Carry no assumptions and have no presumptions about anyone. It is better to use a blank canvas to come up with your own masterpiece, than to paint over someone else's sketches.

4. Growing

The fourth stage is about *Growing* your signature. As an avid gardener, I always use the gardening metaphor here with my onboarding coaching clients. You have planted the seed, you must water it and fertilise it regularly, and keep the weeds away too. This is an important stage in the model where the new recruit pays close attention to the impressions being formed about them in the team. A quick illustration of impression formation and the need to manage it is provided by the following short story.

Noma's story

Noma worked as a marketing specialist for a telecommunications company and had designed, led, driven and successfully delivered numerous marketing accounts with a small team. She was promoted to lead a larger team in one of the fast-growing divisions of the business.

The new team had older, more senior and more experienced yet technologically less-savvy members. One of the challenges Noma was asked to address when she joined this team was to ensure that most of them either got upskilled, reskilled or moved along to make room for bringing in fresh talent that can "dance freely with new technology" as she put it. She soon realised that most of them were stuck in their ways and happy to keep doing what they had been doing all along. She needed to build a new team altogether, with new skills that the company needed for business success.

One of the more vocal members of her new team would always challenge everything she raised about upskilling and taking courses on the use of technology and other innovative or new mobile support tools to increase turn-around times or enhance product quality. Within a few weeks, her twice-weekly team meetings became a battle zone between Noma and her "new" team. She found out she had an unflattering nickname that they had given her. It was something to do with being a hired blue-eyed assassin on behalf of executive management that wanted to get rid of or replace senior employees.

This could all have been avoided had Noma spent a bit more time getting to meet and know each of her new team members, instead of tackling the issues before finding out more about the team. After seven team coaching sessions, a team-building breakaway weekend, and the departure of some of the team members, Noma was able to build (not rebuild) a new team. She is always eager to share her lessons from this experience.

The message from Noma's story for new leaders and managers is not just to meet and greet your new team; it is to seek to connect from the outset. New hires in leadership roles have a responsibility to "see" their team members as they are. There is incredible connective power in being "*seen*" as we are, without the stories that have been shared by others about us.

5. Adjusting

The fifth stage in the Model is *Adjusting*. As the workplace continually changes, it is the leader who is constantly learning who stands a better chance of succeeding. There are lessons to be learned and adapted as the leader, manager or new chief is onboarded and socialised into the work of the team they are joining. This stage is crucial to model a learning approach from the outset, and requires a higher level of vulnerability to self-adjust and self-correct, while also asking for, receiving and taking in the team's feedback. It also means understanding how people experience you as a leader, finding out what their concerns are in working with a new boss, and helping them to understand your expectations of them as their leader. The more they can share in the creation of a new team culture, the sooner new bonds and stronger relationships can help the team to sustain change.

6. Reviewing

The sixth stage is *Reviewing,* and this is another "lessons learned" stage building on the lived adjustments that take place as the work continues. Reviewing is a pause moment the new recruit allows themselves to breathe, while reflecting on how they have done what they have done, in the way that they have done it. This is another honest feedback stage of the model which includes acknowledgment of each other's skill and competence, as well as a willingness to listen to and be influenced by the thinking and feelings of the other members of the team.

7. Developing

The seventh and final stage is *Developing*. It is about identifying and consciously grooming future chiefs. While the seeds for developing new leaders are planted earlier as the team's chief arrives and gets socialised into the work of the organisation, this stage requires that the team start to recognise and support the emerging leaders. There is likely to be more than one team member capable of leading the team, and teams with greater psychological safety find it easy to navigate the developmental phase that requires courage to step up and lead. This is beyond the formal succession plans of the team.

Selected onboarding tips to connect with your team

> "There are truths on one side of the world, which are falsehoods on the other side" – *African proverb.*

This section presents a selection of tips and sets of topics for new leader-managers to use in their first few days, weeks and months with their new team. The rule here is to take what is useful for you and your situation. Not everything fits in with, or is relevant to, every single one of us. Use whatever is usable for you. Leave the rest for later. Enjoy the adventure with your new team.

Ask yourself these fact-finding questions: What exactly is this new role I am starting? What are the details that I am not fully aware of? During the first few weeks, it can be helpful to avoid offering opinions before listening actively and attentively to what the new team is saying. Asking more questions can become informative. New leader-managers can learn from their teams and others around them and share their experiences in a measured manner. The tip is not to smother others with what we know before we understand the context. The following "noticing" tips can be useful:

- *Notice*: Who are the key stakeholders in my operating environment?

- *Notice*: Who relies on my or my team's performance to deliver on their targets?

- *Notice*: Who do I need to regularly engage with to meet my targets? (communication).

- *Notice*: "Headline stories" your new team members are eager to share. The headlines may not always be accurate, or made with positive intent. Remain curious. It helps to take note of the "loudspeakers". Take everything you hear upfront as just input. Nothing is the ultimate truth.

In Organisational Relationship Systems Coaching we work with something called the "2 per cent truth". Everyone owns part of the truth – no one owns all of the truth in any discussion or argument. When you hear something and are convinced that only some of it is possibly true, be willing to hear other divergent points of view to bring in other perspectives. Also, think about what is the "2 per cent truth" when you are given feedback yourself, or about how you are seen and experienced in the team. Look for the "2 per cent truth" to see what you can learn from the feedback.[46]

For new leader-managers, it helps to read every HR file on your team members. Knowing your new team's strengths and areas of development can be powerful. Be cautious around the "eager beavers" who have ready answers for every question you ask. Avoid being "set up" to appear to be supportive of one or other "group". Check everything first. To do this, you need to give yourself sufficient time and space for reflection and analysis.

While remaining curious, it helps to speak up firmly and ask incisive questions when others offer their views. Not everyone will have your best interests at heart right from the start. Be decisive and firm when you need to be, especially when some of your team members were expecting to be appointed to the same position or role you now occupy. Check who wanted your job or role in your team. Yes, you will have to work with them. Can you? What is your plan or strategy to work well with them?

Ideally, first nurture and protect yourself. Manage your workload and energy, and safeguard your space carefully. Most new managers tend to take on too much to impress their new bosses. If you can help it, do not volunteer for too much too quickly. Limit your other involvements to stay focused until you fully grasp your new responsibilities. This includes your non-work-related engagements. Where possible, it helps to find a sounding board, and work with a mentor or a professional coach to help you settle in into your role.

Remember, we are always sending multiple signs and messages we share with those around us, especially when we are either enjoying things or upset and unhappy with any situation. Our energies resonate more powerfully than we often realise.

Hot tips from new leader-managers

The following is a selection of recommendations and tips from new leader-managers with whom I have worked over the years. These tips may not be relevant to all new leader-managers:

- Please say hello! I'm new here. Not being openly welcomed and not even greeted, is one of the worst things to happen to a new hire. It says the place has no heart or soul.

- Induction must happen on the first day I arrive, not days or weeks later. Take me around the office and introduce me to everyone I need to know or that I will work with.

- Help me familiarise myself with the facilities, safety and other areas of interest to make my entry smoother.

- Please do not babysit me. My newness does not mean that I am dumb or slow. Please do not overplay my newness. Do not over-shield me. Let me develop a genuine feel for this place. If it is hostile, I will handle it. You hired me for a reason. Create enough space for me to jump in and swim.

- Allow me to showcase my skills. Let me fail fast, and chances are that I will learn swiftly. As a new leader/manager/employee, I do not plan to be a quick clone.

- Leadership is not a popularity contest. I am not here to become liked and/or popular. I will not try to blend in. I plan to be my own person from the outset.

- Please note that I will not be too quick to buy into the *status quo*. I seek to learn and understand first. I am aware that I am being wooed by different factions, cliques and groups. For now, and maybe even later, I plan to remain independent.

- Sometimes I may not see the lines; I will still try to read between them. It is my intention to pay attention to what is not being said. So, I will remain sceptical. There will be many different narratives at play. I may just create my own. I guarantee you I will check my information repeatedly and verify everything I am told.

- Whatever you do, please do not try to ingratiate yourself with me just because I am the new boss in town. Be real with me. I can smell trouble a mile away, especially from those who try to bad-mouth others and make themselves smell like roses.

Conclusion

This chapter presented a selection of employee socialisation tools and techniques that employers, line managers, human resource practitioners and new employees themselves can utilise to help successfully onboard new hires into their roles, functions and culture of the team or organisational system. The chapter also shared selected employee socialisation and onboarding tools, including selected stages often followed in successful onboarding processes. The latter sections of the chapter presented a socialisation model called RAMGARD that I developed and used over time.

Exercise: Connecting with self and others

Before you can connect to others in your new role, it is important to first understand yourself and your areas of strength and development. Please answer the following questions and share with your team. Then have your team answer the questions, coming prepared to a meeting. Ask each of them to share their own answers with the team:

1. What defines me (beyond my positions, roles and responsibilities)?

2. What are my strengths, talents and gifts that I bring to the team?

3.   What are my areas of development as a team player or team leader?

Chapter 5

Emotional intelligence

This chapter explores the role and power of emotional intelligence in driving engagement within a team and across an organisation. It describes the emotional intelligence qualities needed for rallying employees around a shared goal, and how resonance helps deliver on the collective ambitions of a team or group of employees. Both emotional intelligence and resonance are critical for a leader or manager to build their new team, especially after joining a team or a new organisation. As Goleman points out, "Leadership is not domination, but the art of persuading people to work toward a common goal."[47]

What is emotional intelligence?

My understanding of emotional intelligence is that it is the ability to become – and to stay – aware of our own emotional triggers. It is also the ability to manage our own emotions, alongside managing relationships with others, as they deal with their own emotional states. I believe that resonance is attunement to another as they are, and as they experience others. When we are in resonance, we are in some form of alignment and on the same "wavelength" with others. It has a positive impact. Dissonance is misalignment and not being on the same wavelength. It is like singing out of tune with others; dissonance is like discord in a relationship.

Leaders attuned to others are interested in the collective wellbeing of their people, their teams, and the organisation in which they all serve. They recognise that meaningful success is inherently a collective effort towards the greater good, rather than individual pursuit of limited personal goals. When entering organisational systems, emotionally intelligent managers and leaders understand that they must seek to make solid connections and find resonance with the people in their teams and in the organisation. Parker reminds us that people are emotional beings: "When dealing with people, let us remember we are not dealing with creatures of logic. We are dealing with creatures of emotion, creatures bristling with prejudices and motivated by pride and vanity."[48]

In their seminal work on emotional intelligence and the new leaders, Goleman, Boyatzis and McKee highlight the power of tuning in to others' emotions and feelings. They argue that one of the most critical roles of a leader is "driving the collective emotions in a positive direction and clearing the smog created by toxic emotions. This task applies to leadership everywhere, from the boardroom to the shop floor".[49]

In a *Harvard Business Review* article titled "Primal leadership: The hidden driver of great performance", Goleman, Boyatzis and McKee[50] emphasise the value of creating desired conditions where everyone can express and deploy their talents for the benefit of the team and the organisation. They maintain that:

> High levels of emotional intelligence … create climates in which information sharing, trust, healthy risk-taking, and learning flourish. Low levels of emotional intelligence create climates rife with fear and anxiety. Because tense or terrified employees can be very productive in the short term, their organisations may post good results, but they never last.[51]

One of the greatest early responsibilities of a new recruit joining an existing team, especially in an influential role, is to influence the development and "installation" of a climate conducive to building a high-performance culture. Emotional intelligence, or at least emotional awareness and emotional literacy, are integral to building a new team. These powerful resonance skills assist in building solid teams that are resilient and can withstand and possibly eject negative and toxic new leaders. They can also welcome new members easily without fear of losing themselves.

The above is an integral part of what has been defined as *emotional intelligence*. It encapsulates practices and behaviours – and ways of being – through which leaders handle themselves and their relationships. Goleman et al. add that when leaders "drive emotions positively", they achieve what they call "resonance". It builds strong and resonant teams of employees that help drive and achieve positive performance. The opposite of this is when leaders drive emotions negatively, resulting in disconnection and "dissonance".[52]

The gift of connection with others is strikingly similar to the isiZulu greeting "*Sawubona!*" described in Chapter 6. This practice of attuning ensures that leaders trying to build their new teams are able to connect at a primal level of being humane with their teams or members of their new teams. It leads to situations and scenarios where members of the team refer to the leader as someone who "gets us" or understands them as they are, and does not try to change, turn, or unduly influence them.

Building your new team – through and beyond onboarding – includes this sacred process of "seeing" others as they are. Goleman, Boyatzis and McKee (2002b: 63) describe it as follows: "When leaders are able to grasp other people's feelings and perspectives, they access a potent emotional guidance system that keeps what they say and do on track."

This looks to me like a form of deep empathy. Empathetic leaders ignite good feelings of connection and togetherness in others and with others, and strengthen teaming or group attributes. When applied in lived situations, Ubuntu, empathy, emotional intelligence, social intelligence and resonance all seem to have one common result. They galvanise people in groups or teams, and in whole organisations, to reach for higher or greater collaboration and seek to achieve goals that serve the greater good – and not merely the individual leader or organisational bully and demagogue hiding behind positional role and authority.

Goleman suggests that social intelligence is more than just cognitive intelligence applied to social situations. There is more to it, and this may be understood as "the ability to understand other people and how they will react to different social situations".[53] In my view, social intelligence is a critically important skill for new hires to have, especially in management or leadership roles. Understanding other people is generally a valuable skill for any adult human being to learn and master as they perform their functions in different roles.

Stout-Rostron describes emotions and feelings in the modern workplace as having a bad name:

> In the working world, we tend to think we have to suppress our emotions and feelings – not allowing them to interfere with our rational or logical thinking. However, the way our brain is hardwired, we cannot think without feeling, nor can we feel without thinking.[54]

My contention is that during new employee socialisation processes, such as onboarding and induction, emotions and feelings among new recruits and existing employees can easily get heightened. It is the responsibility of new employees to refine their ways and skills in "reading the room" and quickly learning the new environment's cues, behaviours, language and related behavioural nuances with which older team members are familiar. Failing to read these cues well, and not clearly seeking to know or learn about them early on, can present serious socialisation challenges for the new recruit and their team. Relationships can easily get worse if and when the new recruit is in a leading or managing role and does not pay attention to the team's emotions and feelings.

This issue of being emotionally connected or engaged has also been highlighted by Goleman et al., who emphasise the importance of tuning in to others' emotions:

> Being attuned to how others feel in the moment, a leader can say and do what's appropriate, whether that means calming fears, assuaging anger, or joining in good spirits. This attunement also lets a leader sense the shared values and priorities that can guide the group.[55]

Taking others' emotions and feelings into account is the smart thing to do. Being emotionally aware is not a sign of weakness. It is not what old-school leaders would term "being spineless" or "lacking backbone". Openly expressing, engaging with or attending to others' emotions is regarded as a sign of being emotionally intelligent.

New recruits who show a clear acknowledgement of others' emotions find it easier to build relationships in their new environments than those who ignore team members' feelings, impose themselves on others, and are ego-driven and self-centred in their approach. Leaders lacking in compassion, or better still those with little or no empathy, either create hostile team environments, or lose traction in their efforts to integrate into existing teams or to build their new teams in the new workplace they are joining. Empathy is a leadership superpower.

During employee socialisation or extended onboarding, a new recruit with empathy is likely to connect better, tap into existing norms and values more effectively, more easily access information, and find themselves offered the support they need to build their new team. Goleman et al. contend that "Empathy, which includes listening and taking in other people's perspectives, allows leaders to tune in to the emotional channels between people that create resonance."[56]

Empathy is what global leadership lacks, and what businesses and corporations around the world would do well to embrace and develop. It is exactly what business schools around the world should be teaching:

> ... in the growing global economy, empathy is a critical skill for both getting along with diverse workmates and doing business with people from other cultures. Cross-cultural dialogue can easily lead to miscues and misunderstandings. Empathy is an antidote that attunes people to the subtleties in body language or allows them to hear the emotional message beneath the words.[57]

What I find striking in these works by Goleman et al. is the positioning of emotional intelligence and resonance as critical elements that ignite enthusiasm, positive attitudes and excellence in a team or group of employees. This is even more crucial for a new leader or manager joining an existing team or organisation and seeking to either turn things around or drive performance towards desired and /or expected levels. One of the most important tasks for such a leader is to create, establish or generate resonance in the team they lead.

Another essential ingredient in the challenging work of entry into an organisational system is understanding what your own "emotional style" is, as Goleman et al.

describe it. This refers to the emotional impact the leader has on those around them. The leader's emotional style is either toxic or inspiring.[58]

Heads and hearts in teams

Nancy Kline says that "Teams are now the primary force of organisations. They are worth cultivating at their core. Their core is the mind of each team member."[59] Knowing that Kline includes the heart when she speaks of the mind, I would agree with her that the core of the team is the mind of each member. Kline also says it this way: "Thinking at its best is not just a cool act of cerebration. It is also a thing of the heart."[60]

The context or specific situation being addressed is what shapes and influences the stance of the leader or team making decisions about *how* to proceed. In an ideal scenario, both the heart and mind must inform the final decision and direction a leader takes. These two centres – or spheres – work best together, and can be powerful when mutually reinforcing.

In any team, or any group of people, we get into an unwinnable argument when we try to pit the brain (or mind, thought and the cognitive centre) against the heart (feelings and the emotional centre) without considering the context. Whether a leader must listen more with their heart than they do with their mind tends to be guided by the specific context in which they find themselves, or the particular challenge for which they are seeking solutions. I would not simply say that the leader's heart is far more important than their mind; the context or situation confronting them tends to determine which responses suit the situation. Setting a compelling vision often requires both the head and the heart, especially to ensure that the vision or direction is balanced, cohesive, and makes sense to current and future followers and stakeholders. This stance lays more solid foundations for teaming and transformational inclusiveness than one that relies solely on either of the two centres of influence.

If, however, I were compelled to choose a preferred working approach and perspective on the above, I would say that that the mind-sets of the leader and team or group are less critical to the development and growth of the team than the heart-sets of the leader, the team and the organisation.

Meetings that enhance connection in the new normal

"Listening … ignites the human mind. The quality of your listening determines the quality of other people's thinking".[61]

What is a meeting? How do we distinguish between great and terrible meetings? How about exciting versus boring meetings? In the working world today, meetings tend to take over all the thinking space and time in a team. Running an effective meeting is a primary skill for success for any leader-manager.

There are numerous types of meeting. Meetings are purpose-filled gatherings that can take place in-person, virtually, or be hybrid or mixed (part-virtual, with some participants attending in person and others connecting virtually).

One of the most important lessons I have gathered from my experience running meetings as a team leader and as a manager has been the value of giving everyone a fair chance or turn to share their views. I learned this early in my life from watching elders during meetings in the rural village where I grew up, and closely observing my grandfathers and my father leading the community in deliberations. I have since had the privilege of running such meetings myself, and was filled with pride when after one such meeting, two grey-haired, elderly men openly commended my manner of running the meeting, especially *"ukwamukela onke amazwi nemibono"* (welcoming every voice and opinion).

The above scenarios take place in many locations around the world, and they do not get written about as much as boardroom scenarios and engagements. Nancy Kline's well-documented way of running meetings makes clear sense, and the village elders would approve! It is certainly a tried and tested way that seems to work every time. I have seen and experienced this across the spectrum, and can attest to Kline's point that "Giving everyone a turn increases the intelligence of the group ... [and] Knowing they won't be interrupted frees people to think faster and say less".[62]

As a practising one-to-one and team coach, some of my clients have asked me to share tools for managing meetings more effectively than just running through a long agenda and hearing their own voice over and over. One of my favourite references on the subject of conducting effective meetings has been Nancy Kline's Thinking Environment, especially the Ten Components of a Thinking Environment, as follows:

1. *Attention*: Listening without interruption and with interest in where the person will go next in their thinking.

2. *Incisive questions*: Freeing the human mind of an untrue assumption lived as true.

3. *Equality*: Regarding each other as thinking peers, giving equal time to think.

4. *Appreciation*: Noticing what is good and saying it.

5. *Ease*: Discarding internal urgency.

6. *Encouragement*: Giving courage to go to the unexplored edge of thinking by ceasing competition as thinkers.

7. *Feelings*: Welcoming the release of emotion.

8. *Information*: Supplying facts, recognising social context, dismantling denial.

9. *Place*: Producing a physical environment – the room, the listener, your body – that says, "You matter."

10. *Difference:* Championing our inherent diversity of identity and thought.[63]

The Ten Components of a Thinking Environment can create an atmosphere where everyone feels both valuable and able to co-create desired solutions. This is particularly important for new employees to feel welcome and accepted into the team or organisational system.

During new-employee socialisation and onboarding engagements, it helps if new hires feel that they can freely express themselves and do not need to search hard for opportunities to speak up in meetings or other engagement sessions. This is especially important when organisational or team leaders intend to build inclusive, open, engaging or coaching cultures in which all members of the team or organisational system feel included and valued.

One of the reasons for highlighting these meeting pointers and qualities is the important role and value of meetings and other engagement platforms in encouraging and building team coherence and co-creating dynamic, high-performance cultures. This starts with genuine connection. Real, authentic connection happens in the shared spaces, whether intentionally created or random, where old and new employees encounter each other. Formal meetings present such platforms.

The "P" stance for leaders in meetings

This section reproduces material from an article previously published in *Business Essentials*, by permission of the publisher.[64]

"P" stands for "Pause". The purpose of this is to pause and make sure in a meeting you bring everyone on board with you – sometimes you don't need to include the entire agenda. This thought was inspired by attending too many boring and energy-sapping meetings, and recognising how much time (and money!) could be saved by making meetings not only shorter and sharper, but more productive and inspiring. We refer to "Pausing" as a practice to listen – and to connect! This is a core attention practised in our work with leaders and in the training and growth towards maturity. The embodiment of being mindful, reflective and considered comes into being. The result is a more skilful and conscious action, and is core to being an effective intervener within our own lives and through others.

The "P" stance for leaders during meetings refers to the need for leaders, managers, and anyone running a meeting to develop a higher level of awareness which ensures they are effective in inviting everyone's voice into their meeting. This is a powerful tool with potential to change how meetings are conducted, and improve the outcomes of those meetings! The "P" stance draws from some of Nancy Kline's tools for managing meetings, especially the Thinking Environment. Another tool that has informed the "P" stance is the ancient African method of conducting meetings, which in Southern Africa has variations that include the *lekgotla* or *inkundla*. A similar tool is the "Talking Stick". In the *lekgotla* and Thinking Environment, the leader of the meeting ensures that the occasion is not about themselves, but about listening and hearing all the voices present in the meeting.

The "P" stance provides a step-by-step guide, especially to the new leader-manager, on how to get the most out of each meeting. It is part of a suite of tools used by seasoned facilitators, leaders, coaches and managers to empower others in the meeting. This tool helps unleash the inherent human excellence already within all of us. It is a systems tool informed by the values and principles of Ubuntu.

Here are the seven steps of the "P" stance:

Step 1: Shut up (yes, zip it!): ... and stop thinking about what to say next. Be deeply silent and ready to really hear – and hear – more than is said through the mouth. Breathe in deeply, and be quiet. Observe the one speaking and connect with them. Notice. Sense. Be fully engaged. Quietly.

Step 2: Listen with your whole being: When we are truly silent and in *present pause,* most if not *all* our senses open up for us to listen with our *whole* being. What is your gut feel saying? You are more than your intellect. Make sure you take many deep breaths. Your body knows better. Listen to it.

Step 3: Hear everything, including what is not being said: Notice what the speaker's whole body is saying. When someone speaks, how is the rest of the room or audience responding to them? Learn more about body language.

Step 4: Ask the right questions: We often ask questions whose answers we already know. Before you ask each question, ask yourself what you want to achieve with the possible responses to that question. It must serve the collective and not you or your preferred stance in the meeting. Notice whether you have favourite questions, and what your body says as you ask your questions. Notice where your eyes are as you ask your questions. Connect.

Step 5: Check in with others before expressing your views: Before you offer your views or opinions, check in with those who have not offered their views in the session. Invite them in. Continue in your stance and listen more.

Step 6: Share your informed and balanced view: Finally, after your intentional deep listening, you may now "press play" and offer an informed and (hopefully) balanced view. Remember, while it is not all about you, as the leader, you must take responsibility and be fully accountable for the output and outcome of the meeting. It is *you and your team's* meeting. Speak with your whole being and from a stance of authentic, values-based leadership. Meetings, or any human gatherings, should never be drowned by the same voices and opinions all the time. Whenever we think that the person who is quiet or silent in the room has nothing to say, or judge and label them in any way, we have lost part of the plot. Use the "P" stance to invite everyone in. You will be glad you did.

Step 7: Acknowledge with gratitude: Yes, say "thank you" and mean it. People know when a "thank you" is fake. Make sure it is both genuine and heartfelt. It can be magical. And keep your meetings short. Always.

It is well known that in order to build effective leadership skills and attributes, new or younger leaders need to learn listening skills and put these vital tools to good use regularly, daily and consistently.

In the next section of the chapter, we encounter the story of new hires trying hard to make a connection and failing to listen carefully, and the lessons emanating from that. The lesson in the case illustration below is that leaders need to learn to listen, listen, listen, and listen some more – to just about everyone.

A story of onboarding mistakes and misreading connection cues

At 38, Lebo felt that he was on top of his game. Any game, but more importantly, the business game. Not only did he feel that he was physically fit and healthy, he also felt like he was in the prime of his mental capacities and a rising star in the corporate ladder of international business. Yet the call that Lebo received was totally unexpected.

A multinational consulting firm had head-hunted him and felt that he was ready for the big league. They wanted an energetic young executive to head up their

Corporate Affairs Department, and had specifically asked the search companies to look for someone who was youngish, versatile, personable and able to learn fast.

The new executive role was too attractive to turn down. Lebo jumped at the opportunity. He signed up for his most senior, most lucrative and most challenging role yet.

Lebo's office was the proverbial corner one. A great desk with leather trim, a comfortable swivelling tan-coloured leather chair, and a matching leather office lounge suite, with a television set connected via satellite to channels such as Bloomberg and CNBC broadcasting the latest business news. His Executive Assistant was a sharply-dressed young man in his early thirties, well-spoken and efficient in just about everything he touched. He loved his job. Lebo immediately felt assured that he was in good hands.

As soon as his new boss had briefed him, and he had received his working tools, including the latest, brand-new, shiny laptop, Lebo met with his HR business partner to brief him in detail about his team. Lebo scheduled meetings with his team of direct reports (all managers) for the first week of his onboarding. He wanted to meet first with the manager who had been acting in his (Lebo's) new job. He felt that this would give him a good grasp of the role. The 55-year-old HR business executive, seemingly concerned, suggested that Lebo meet first with some support staff, and then some of the senior professionals, before meeting his group of four managers. Lebo did not see the value of this; he wanted to "go straight to the business end of knowing what we do here".

This was a huge mistake.

The first person Lebo met was the manager who had acted in his new job. Surely there could be no landmines or slippery slopes in taking this well-considered step, right? Surely not.

What Lebo was not told was that the manager (we shall call him Jimmy; an equally driven chartered accountant with executive ambitions of his own), had wanted the executive role so badly that he had even tried to find out more about the job specifications when the advert was being prepared by HR. His stint acting in the role had emboldened him into thinking that the job was in the bag. However, his poor interrelationship and limited people skills had persuaded the Managing Director to look elsewhere. HR was thus instructed to look externally for fresh executive talent.

Lebo had seen everyone's HR file, and did not pick up any red lights at all; everyone looked "good for their roles". So here was Lebo, sitting on his new leather couch with the heir apparent to his job and the very person who had lost out. Lebo had no idea that Jim had applied for the post, let alone the fact that he had not even been shortlisted for interviews!

Could this be an onboarding banana peel for Lebo? How was he going to navigate it?

Lebo and Jimmy shook hands like normal businesspeople did before COVID-19. There were all smiles in the room. Lebo's Executive Assistant asked Jimmy what he would like to drink during the meeting. "Coffee with milk, please, thank you." The Executive Assistant already knew what Lebo was going to have. I did say he was on top of his office game, right? Right.

As they sat down, leather couch squeaking somewhat, Lebo started: "So, Jim, tell me more about yourself …"

Case illustrations and stories such as the one above present valuable lessons for engagement and genuine connection. The tools for engagement are given free expression through positive energy that is best created by leaders with a vision for authentic relationship building and getting the best out of every member of their team.

Conclusion

This chapter dealt with the important human connection qualities of emotional intelligence in shared spaces such as organisations and workplaces. Leaders with emotional intelligence are able to identify and manage their own and others' emotions. Such leaders have the advantage of their emotional intelligence ability not to be reactive to situations with tension. Such leaders are also capable of avoiding getting triggered by tensions and hostility. Many emotionally intelligent leaders, be they old or new to their roles, can carefully assess human engagement situations and choose appropriate responses that benefit their relationships with new members joining their teams. Emotionally intelligent leaders can effectively strengthen their teams through the emotionally intelligent ways they use to engage with their new members. Such leaders can easily build resonance and authentic connections that help their new hires or teams quickly settle into their roles and feel part of the organisational ecosystem. Emotional intelligence sets the tone, pace and example for high-performance teams and cultures in organisations.

This chapter also explored meetings and related gatherings as focal points for enhancing individual and team connection. Meetings can provide the best stage for new employees to share and showcase what they bring to the team and organisational system. When they are well-managed, inclusive and open, meetings can be powerfully energising units of connection and engagement. They have the potential to galvanise teams and even whole organisational systems, and raise employee morale. Great meetings may even lead to new employees finding their feet quicker and making contributions with less fear than when meetings are bullying arenas where leaders are mini-dictators who do not understand the value of the Thinking Environment or the "P" stance in meetings.

Exercise: My connection qualities

Answer the following question:

1. What unique qualities do I bring when first connecting with others?

Complete the following statements:

2. My human connection blind spots are …

3. The connection qualities that I admire most in other people are …

Exercise: Power listening to connect

Answer the following questions:

1. What distracting behaviours do I display in other people's meetings – and even in mine?

2. What are my development areas or blind spots when listening to others?

3. What do I need to change to be a better listener and contributor in meetings?

Chapter 6

Ubuntu coaching

What is Ubuntu?

"Ubuntu is best understood experientially".[65]

Ubuntu is a word commonly used among the Nguni ethnic groups spread across southern Africa. In SeSotho, which is one of the most commonly spoken languages in southern Africa and the language spoken in Lesotho, this concept of Ubuntu is called *botho*. It is a way of being, a manner of engagement, and a worldview that is often used when referring to the natural humaneness, goodness and inherent interconnectedness of human beings with each other. Ubuntu means *I am because we are, and you are because we are*. It means that I cannot be fully me if you cannot be fully you.

The practice of Ubuntu means that if I can express myself to the best of my abilities, and you cannot, then we are both not truly "free". If I am not enabling you to be the best version of you, and especially if I am actively obstructing you from becoming everything you can be, then by implication I am robbing myself of the gifts that you came here to deliver and share through your life.

One of the strongest proponents of Ubuntu in business and within communities, Dr Reuel Khoza, describes Ubuntu as the view that a person can only really become a person through others:

> In Africa we say a person is a person because of other people, and nowhere is this more apt than in the relationship between leader and followers. Moral dependence is the ethic of African humanism, or Ubuntu. In its strongest formulation, it asserts that my very being derives from yours, and yours from all of us.[66]

It is this conceptual foundation of Ubuntu that makes it more suitable to organisational and team leadership now during the virtual world of work than ever before. When this approach is adopted by new recruits coming into teams and organisations to lead or manage others, they have a much greater chance of success than other strictly transactional approaches that offer a trade-off between leader and follower.

Ubuntu levels the playing field, while strengthening collective accountability. This does not, however, preclude the individual from their specific personal responsibility and accountability. It merely places greater value on the collective or the greater good than on individual importance. The collective is greater than the individual. The individual is accountable to the collective and must ensure that they give of their best for the benefit of the collective and not for their selfish individual needs. This approach is suitable for building new organisational teams.

Ubuntu values and Ubuntu awareness is about heightening our awareness of the collective or the greater good. Ubuntu is about being selfless, as opposed to being selfish and self-centred. Living with Ubuntu values does not mean that we do not think about ourselves. It means that we think about ourselves and about others, and that we think about our impact on others in context. Ubuntu as a way of being is needed now more than ever before in an increasingly technologically interconnected world, where fellow humans find themselves increasingly disconnected and out of touch with what makes humans humane.

The capital accumulation, greed and avarice of multinational corporations, alongside predatory practices of many businesses and some nations, makes the call for greater human interconnectedness ever more urgent. The quotation below presents the case aptly:

> A worldwide trend of disconnection and alienation leads to the dire consequences of losing our connection to source, to nature, to spirit, to each other's humanity and creates the ultimate split: the split of complete separation in which an egoic-self can madly engage in the most psychotic acts of inner and outer violence and degradation.[67]

Khoza maintains that Ubuntu and a humane approach towards navigating our shared spaces is something that can be used anywhere in the world. He argues that "Our humaneness equips us for mutual understanding and communication. We are truly capable of empathising and cooperating across the barriers that have divided humanity".[68]

These barriers to which Khoza is referring are often well-constructed historical perspectives or narratives about each other (or often "the others") that have for a long time served to separate and divide humanity. They include racial and other learned prejudices. They are perpetuated as stereotypes that often serve narrow and limited – and effectively limiting – purposes of some groups over others.

The separating or divisive narrative that Khoza[69] refers to can be found in many so-called modern organisations and workplaces which emphasise individual performance over collective accountability. The organisational challenges of poor team cohesion, limited engagement and lack of recognition of everyone's inherent value are especially heightened when a new team member comes on board seeking to build a new team.

New leaders are always urged to sharpen their personal and leadership antennae to help them pick up all the necessary cues from their new team. They can do this by talking less and listening more to their new team members or followers. A great organisational leader communicates openly and is transparent. The idea or practice of seeking to hear every voice builds great team spirit and team cohesion, and encourages everyone to bring the best of themselves into the team.

The Ubuntu approach to organisational engagement and cohesion supports the building of a new team by engendering trust and honesty in the group. When the leader openly engages with the team using Ubuntu, it is easier to build rapport and resonance with most team members. A leader who leads with Ubuntu is often more emotionally available and accessible to everyone than a leader who Goleman calls the "Office Tyrant". The team leader who leads from an Ubuntu approach has no favourites, nor do they encourage the formation of factions or cliques.

It is not too far-fetched to believe that the Ubuntu approach to organisational work can help leaders anywhere around the world to build the strongest teams possible. Ubuntu is understated and underrated in how it helps shape and impact collaboration in shared environments that require human cooperation. The following quotation from Khoza sums this up quite effectively:

> Africa has a fundamental moral contribution to make to principles of leadership in the world today. Despite the chaos of Africa itself, its philosophical tradition is a respectable one that brings a special perspective to issues of authority, integrity, efficacy and governance. This perspective is humaneness: the idea that we are all sprung from the same evolutionary roots and all contend with the same human condition of birth, struggle and death.[70]

As people, we have a whole lot more in common than what separates us. The challenge that Ubuntu helps us attend to is seeing each other as on the same human team. I have always maintained that Ubuntu is a global phenomenon, and one of which the world needs to be reminded.[71]

The message from Khoza[72] above reiterates this point emphatically: Ubuntu or humaneness is what the world needs more now than ever before, and the modern workplace is one of the shared spaces where this must play out now. The starting point for most organisational players seeking humane connection to achieve this broad and necessary global transformation is the leader's heart, followed by the team through which the leader serves, and then the organisation within which the leader leads.

Vuyisile Msila, in his book *Ubuntu: Shaping the current workplace with African wisdom*, says that "the values embraced by Ubuntu are the missing links in dysfunctional workplaces" (Msila, 2015: 6). This explains the disconnection and dissonance found within many organisations around the world. This is also experienced by multiple teams searching for cohesion and other teaming attributes.

The dysfunction Msila[73] refers to is what the new team leader finds as the main obstacle in efforts to build their team. Ubuntu represents the much-sought-after and yet consistently elusive solution to this challenge. The best part of this approach or perspective is that Ubuntu is both versatile and flexible enough to be fully applicable wherever humans find themselves needing to collaborate.

Willem de Liefde says that modern organisations need to shift away from the classic Western way of thinking that places the primacy of the individual at the heart of the business. He says that this approach of making the individual – instead of the group – the focal point creates mistrust.[74] De Liefde maintains that "By once more placing the interests of the group foremost, managers (innovators) give back self-respect to employees."[75]

Whether the leader or manager is building the new team from the ruins and smouldering embers of an old one, or setting it up from scratch, it is crucial to ensure that the group, team or collective *sees* and *feels* that the team leader sees, recognises and acknowledges them as vital stakeholders in the new team.

Human beings tune in into each others' energy. Where there is already great connection, the team can *sense* and somehow *know* when the team leader is faking connection, empathy and compassion. In my experience, the best stance is for the new leader or manager to remain both authentic and vulnerable. This enables the team to be authentic and vulnerable too, especially with the new leader, who would then use the genuine interconnections to build their new team with new values and positively impact the working culture going forward.

The modern world of work is dominated by businesses that are run through organisations. Organisations are human ecosystems that can often be regarded as living entities themselves. In the shared spaces within these living organisations, it is our mutual responsibility to ensure that everyone is able – and free – to express themselves fully *as they are*. If one or some of us are not able to be fully themselves, that means we all fall short of being fully humane.

Understanding Ubuntu coaching

Before delving deeper into the value of Ubuntu in creating your new team, this section shares some thoughts and reflections on Ubuntu coaching. The emerging and fresh African framework called Ubuntu coaching is gaining traction among some forward-thinking coaching practitioners and coach training institutions in South Africa and the sub-Saharan region of the continent.

Ubuntu can be easily described as being responsive to the inherent qualities of "humaneness" already within us, or as the ability to be consistently humane, warm and loving when dealing with or relating to fellow humans regardless of their station in life, position or role within an organisation or community. Ubuntu emphasises that we are inherently interconnected, and that *I am because we are.* Ubuntu means that what I am is a result of who we are as humans. In other words, what I am and what I do impacts you and the next person. In turn, what you do has implications for me and others too. We must therefore care about what the other does.

One of my favourite descriptions of Ubuntu is the one given by Archbishop Emeritus of Cape Town, Desmond Tutu, when he said:

> Africans have a thing called Ubuntu. It is about the essence of being human. It is part of the gift that Africa is going to give to the world. It embraces hospitality, caring about others, being willing to go the extra mile for the sake of another. We believe that a person is a person through other persons; that my humanity is caught up and bound up in yours. When I dehumanise you, I inexorably dehumanise myself. The solitary human being is a contradiction in terms, and therefore you seek to work for the common good because your humanity comes into its own in community, in belonging.[76]

Recent developments in the growing field of climate change and environmental challenges, together with the financial crises that the world is struggling to come out of, scream this message at humanity, yet we continue to act in our small configurations called nation-states. Humanity or the human race as we know it today cannot afford to continue thinking, planning and acting in mini-silos called national interests. We must all think and act systemically with the global perspective in mind.

"Ubuntu coaching" refers to the active application of Ubuntu values, Ubuntu principles, and Ubuntu ways of being, in the professional field of business, executive and leadership coaching. It can be used in all modalities of human development such as talent management in business, performance coaching, mentoring, executive development, and other forms of people-management. It is inherently a systems-based meta-model of coaching that both demands and enables leaders to see, appreciate and work with the systems in which they find themselves operating. Ubuntu coaching affords coaches the opportunity to adjust their outlook on business and their leadership approaches. Effective leaders and managers understand that they must start with their close personal relationships and extend this engagement out to their teams and the broader organisation, and beyond to the community and to national and global interests.

Ubuntu coaching involves the people-centric and active re-development of our inherent human ability and capacity to be here (present) and engage authentically with others, as they explore aspects of their lives in what to me is a sacred coaching relationship with a coach. This becomes even more sacred when the client is being enrolled into their new role in an organisation. Ubuntu coaching is therefore the igniting of human potential through in-the-moment recognition of the greatness that is already within the other. The connection process through Ubuntu coaching involves guided presencing questions and awareness that in the moment of interaction we are modelling our ability and capacity to constantly recognise our inherent human interconnectedness. We are illustrating how others should relate to us or treat us.

Successful Ubuntu coaching enables us to live and work with conscious awareness that everything is connected, and to actively connect with fellow beings on a mutual recognition footing. It is the acknowledgement that life is sustained and enriched through these inextricable human interconnections. When we experience Ubuntu coaching, we realise that we were never alone in the first place. Genuine human interconnection enlarges us and helps us become great from within, without relying on external affirmations. Ubuntu coaching is systemic and systems-based, and is inherently inter-relational in form and practice.

Ubuntu coaching requires new mind-sets and uses new heart-sets that enable us to see the self in the other. Most importantly, Ubuntu coaching helps us feel and experience genuine empathy and connection with our fellow human beings. Ubuntu coaching reconnects the channels to our essential natural selves and assists us to get back in sync with all of life and to be in balance within ourselves and with each other. It helps us come back home to our inherent wisdom of knowing that we are interconnected. While this can be tough and challenging for many new leaders who have embodied positional roles and separation from the rest of the team as the norm over time, it can be absolutely exhilarating when fully achieved and recognised as the way to be.

Coaches are allowed to dream too, right? And sometimes dreams do come true. So, let me share one of my dreams with you. This is a part of my Ubuntu leadership coaching dream that helps new employees to be socialised effectively into their new roles:

> *I see a world where all global leaders in politics, business, civil society, the military, multilateral agencies, non-profit organisations, and across many communities, are living and relating to each other in an engaged and engaging systemic manner. Everyone lives and approaches their businesses and their roles from an Ubuntu perspective. There is no egotistical bullying of smaller businesses or countries, and there is genuine global inclusivity in crafting trade regulations and internationally applicable business laws. I see a situation where there is little room for wars, social strife and displacement of large populations through avoidable conflict. There is far less greed and looting of natural resources. There is more dialogue and engagement across the globe, with little discrimination based on perceptions of being less developed, less educated, or just less than. There are no visa requirements to visit friends across any and all international borders. The human race is one big, sometimes happy family!*

I think this dream is possible. It seems quite feasible to me. For now, it remains just a dream. Yet, we can work towards it together.

If all coaches, human resource practitioners, and organisational leaders developed Ubuntu coaching skills in their initial and ongoing professional development, most organisations would move closer to this utopian dream. If we look at it closely, it is not dissimilar to the dreams of visionary leaders like Nelson Mandela, Desmond Tutu, Mother Theresa, the Dalai Lama, Martin Luther King Jnr, and many other *selfless* leaders from around the world. It is essentially humanity's ideal way of co-existing with fellow beings, and with nature, in less judgmental and divisive ways.

The question then becomes: *How* do we bring this about in our chosen vision of Ubuntu coaching? My preliminary answer to this question is that we address it through the introduction of *Ubuntu intelligence* (UbuQ). Ubuntu intelligence is the ability to constantly recognise our human interconnectedness in everything we think, feel and do. It requires new mind-sets and especially new "heart-sets" that help us see ourselves in others. This is especially important when the leader seeks to establish connection and build a new team in the workplace. Heart-sets can be described as ways of being, behaviours, approaches and attitudes, which are guided by seeking to connect with others and serve the collective or the greater good, and not the individual. It is about being selfless and focusing on the team, as opposed to being selfish and thinking and acting only on individual interests. Heart-sets encapsulate the stance of a leader, manager or new recruit positioning themselves to build their new team.

It is about making substantive and real changes in how we relate first to ourselves and then to each other, outside the boxes we create to simplify our understanding of each other in our beautiful diversity. Ubuntu intelligence is the capacity to be genuinely interested in the other without scratching the egotistical itch of wanting to be seen to be better or doing more than the other. It is transcending the shallow personal gratification of material acquisition and other superficial, ephemeral or temporary achievements. It is about authentic, selfless connection and service to others, and to humanity.

My preliminary suggestions and thoughts on this were that as coaches working within organisations, we can rally every coach across the world and spread the power and value of Ubuntu coaching in changing the world. We can nudge every single leader we coach towards greater connection and engagement with their teams. This would be done by raising all coached leaders' awareness of the inherent human capacity to connect to other humans, other beings, and to nature.

Ubuntu coaching is about helping us all *remember* our inherent interconnectedness, and is meant to trigger our natural capacity to tune in into each other in a caring and less aggressive or less self-serving or selfish way. This is already happening in communities where people choose to care for each other with little to share among themselves, while billions of dollars' worth of food is thrown away as waste or as unwanted extras across the more wealthy regions of the world, and sometimes in wealth enclaves in some of the poorer countries in the world.

Coming back to organisations, one example of *how* we can impact the world through Ubuntu coaching is through transforming organisational cultures. Recently we used Ubuntu coaching in the introduction and development of a new organisational culture for one of our clients, with amazingly positive results, especially in employee engagement and connection across structural levels and roles, and across functions. This approach is fast becoming a much-sought-after model for team coaching, employee engagement, and building dynamic coaching cultures in transformative organisations.

Our next challenge is to document clear case studies and share them far and wide to showcase how powerful Ubuntu coaching can be.

In *The Future of Management*, Gary Hamel argues that organisations need management innovation more than ever, because the management paradigm of the twentieth century, which focused on control and efficiency, is no longer sufficient now that business success is driven by adaptability and creativity. Consequently, in order to thrive, companies need to reinvent management.[77]

Beyond *sawubona*: seeing others and being SEEN

Ubuntu coaching is about supporting the client by being grounded in the spirit and sense of being-ness, and not living in our heads or focusing on the rational-logical perspective. One of its leading practitioners is Nobantu Mpotulo MCC, whose perspective is focused on the in-person practice and presence of the coach while engaging in Ubuntu coaching. It is an elegant process, which she starts with an emphasis on meeting and receiving the client through greeting.

Mpotulo's emerging Ubuntu coaching model is predicated on profound presence and connecting authentically to others as they are and where they are. The RASEA steps used in the model constitute a powerful tool for coaching from an Ubuntu systems perspective that is directly informed by the Ubuntu philosophy:

* *receive* the client;

* *appreciate and acknowledge* the client;

* *summarise* what you hear the client saying;

* *evoke* awareness; and

* *ask questions* to move the client to action.[78]

In isiZulu, the most widely-spoken African language in southern Africa, when we meet someone new or an acquaintance we have not seen for some time, we say out loud *"Sawubona!"*. This is a powerful greeting, which literally means "I see you". It initiates genuine human connection and genuine interest in the other. This manner of seeing others means that we see them and receive them as they present themselves, and without our preconceptions or learned narratives about them. Seeing others as they present themselves is a precursor and preparation for us to then hear them as they engage with us in whatever form or language they use. The magic of this human connection starts with seeing the other.

In Mpotulo's training sessions, the participants work with the ability to "see" others as they are in the present moment. The group undertakes an exercise on being seen, delving into what happens when coaches see their clients fully and clearly as they are, with no presumptions. Mpotulo's Ubuntu coaching model emphasises connection, and reiterates that "seeing" another as they are is a gift to both individuals interacting and the community they live and interact within.[79]

In my work with organisational leaders, and while doing personal reflections on the most common practices that had yielded tangible results, I developed a new concept of what happens when we are truly SEEN from an Ubuntu coaching perspective – the SEEN Model, which consists of the following four components:

1. *Safety*. Safety leads to trust and open engagement. The Ubuntu coach engages safely to create the sacred container where the client feels safe enough to explore whatever they are bringing into the coaching engagement … safely connecting.

2. *Engagement*. Ubuntu coaches seek to connect with their clients in a way that enables them to see each other. This is done through genuine engagement. Great engagement enables the coach to see and hear the client clearly and with no judgement.

3. *Embrace*. Embracing others stems from both seeing and hearing them as they express themselves. Embracing others as they are, is profound when we acknowledge and connect with them authentically. The idea here is to notice our filters. It is not a physical embrace. It is a genuine acceptance and connection that facilitates *seeing* and hearing each other deeply ... as we are.

4. *Nurture*. The act of seeing another as they are and hearing them expressing themselves freely is nurturing. When we greet consciously, we nurture and nourish the connections and relationships we have with others. When this is accompanied by genuinely seeing and hearing them as they present themselves in their unique ways, the relationship matures greatly.

Being SEEN is grounded in the ability of the Ubuntu coach to help the client feel safe, held, understood and supported or nurtured. Does everyone yearn to be seen, or want to be seen by others? While I believe that humans are "heart-wired" to connect to each other, I am not sure whether it is true that we are hardwired to want to be seen? How about being heard? Is it natural to human beings to desire being seen and heard? Is it inherently part of human nature to desire this connection? To be really seen as we are is a gift by those that see us, to them and to our connection with them. Seeing others enriches the relationship of the seen and the one seeing. It also invites us to see each other. The next stage of seeing others is tuning in to them and their energy as they are.

Few things as are as affirming, assuring and nurturing of our relationships with others as their ability to notice our roles, gifts and talents, as their ability to really see and hear us as we are. This makes greeting so much more powerful as a process and action to ignite genuine human connection that leads to fulfilling relationships. My hope is that more people in different contexts start to seriously work on genuine connection and become more vulnerable to let others in, or at least lower their guard.

New hires in management and leadership roles carry a larger and more urgent responsibility to find the balance between leading, managing and learning, while sharing what they know has worked elsewhere. In the digital age, the challenge takes on a new urgency in that the new team has access to alternative sources of knowledge and information. The team does not rely on the manager and/or leader to feed them with the latest information in the form of updates.

The advent of working from home, and the normalisation of the virtual world of work, means that they can access knowledge and information for them to remain effective without the manager or leader looking over their shoulder in the shared office space. This then means that the new manager or leader must be flexible, available and agile in maintaining management and leadership authority and guiding the team where they need support. The locus of management and leadership effectiveness has shifted from information access to interrelationship management.

Introducing intempathy

In some of my work with members of economically vulnerable communities, especially youth, I have used practices and engagements that can be best described as "intempathy". *Intempathy* refers to *live and intense empathy* in practice and action. Intempathy is the act or practice of consciously and intensely focusing on sensing what another person is feeling and then acting on it to support them in the moment (as opposed to *sterile empathy* of words or empty gestures with no action to help another). It involves seeking to appreciate how a fellow human being feels in the moment, and what to do to assuage pain or suffering.

Intempathy is consciously going beyond stepping into another person's shoes. It involves *stepping into their heart-sets*, their feelings, their sensitivities in the moment. It also involves *being intensely attuned* to a fellow being as they process and/or deal with something that affects them intensely and requires the support and emotional availability of others in the moment. For new leader-managers, intempathy can be overwhelming if not used carefully. It helps when the new leader-manager first seeks to understand the environment and context fully before deploying intempathy.

Timing is essential in intempathy. It is not something that can be postponed or put off for a convenient time later. Unlike hyper-empathy or what has been termed "over-empathy" or "toxic empathy", intempathy is both positive and other-centred. It is based on or informed by Ubuntu values and is part of the spirit of living with and exhibiting Ubuntu intelligence (UbuQ). I have often called it *Ubuntu mindfulness* in action; it makes better sense that way.

Conscious greetings to ignite genuine connection

Sawubona! Jambo! Molo! Dumelang! Nǐ hǎo! Konnichiwa! Salam! Makadii! Hello! Hi!

- What is in a greeting?

- What is evoked in us when someone greets us?

- Does it raise our level of curiosity? Does it annoy or irritate us?

- Greet all the time ... but *how* exactly?

- Do we greet everyone we meet? Not always. Why is that?

- Do we even greet consciously? Well, what does that really mean?

- Do we at least greet enthusiastically, like we mean it? Sometimes.

- Does greeting make us interesting to others?

- How genuinely interested in others are we?

- What does the way we greet say about us?

The statements and questions above are part of a reflection tool I often use with some of my clients when working on "conscious greetings" (greetings with clear intent, meaning and awareness). Every positive effort to connect authentically and genuinely with everyone we meet starts with a "conscious greeting".

Greeting others consciously is a super-power. It is a wise practice to learn, and to keep greeting others consciously as standard practice or a well-honed habit. Conscious greetings can nourish any relationship and enrich careers. Additionally, it can open up useful channels for engagement between us and the members of our new team with whom we would like to build good relationships. While greetings are often underrated in their power to establish strong connections, we cannot deny that they can be icebreakers in many relationships.

Exercise: Conscious greeting

This exercise can be done in an office building, or in the park, in a shopping mall, on the street, or just about anywhere where there are human beings! It takes courage for some people, while it can be quite easy for others. Know that it can be difficult at first, and simply takes practice.

1. As you walk in a public place, identify someone with whom you can engage – anyone at all – and approach them.

---

2. When – and if – you feel safe to do so, greet them in a way you feel comfortable with.

3. Maintain a friendly demeanour, nothing creepy. Just be a normal, curious human being.

4. If possible, explain what you are doing and why you are doing it (it takes away the awkwardness!).

5. Appreciate the other person for the gift of "conscious greeting".

Tip: This exercise tends to work better when we approach people older than us.

Connection tools for transformational coaches

This section reproduces material from an article previously published in *COACH Magazine*, by permission of the publisher.[80]

As explained in this chapter, when *amaZulu* (Zulu people) in southern Africa meet and greet others they say *"Sawubona!"*, which translates literally as "I see you". It means I see you as you are, or as you present yourself. The idea is that I do not see my presumptions, my learned or borrowed narratives of you, or whatever stories have been written, told and believed about you.

Coaches love to establish great rapport upfront with clients, as good rapport lays a solid foundation for a great coaching relationship. Rapport is the pre-curser to that critical stage of any coaching relationship, the coaching contract. It prepares the ground for what Nancy Kline calls the Thinking Environment.[81] In a Thinking Environment, everyone's voice is sacred, and when others are "seen" and listened to, they can think clearly. There is psychological safety in being authentic. All human beings deserve that. This way, we can all breathe freely.

A genuine *sawubona* greeting offers both parties a "sacred opportunity to see each other as they are". The lingering human challenge many coaches wrestle with, is that most people do not really "see" each other as they are. We tend to see more the story we have come to believe about the "other", rather than a fellow human being right in front of us. This becomes even more crucial when the "other" happens to be from a "different" culture or ethnic group than our own.

The world we operate in as coaches and human development practitioners is increasingly unpredictable and fluid, especially with fast-changing mobile technologies that connect us wherever we are. Most professional and business coaches understand that coaching is inherently contextual.

Coaching contexts constantly fluctuate and throw up hitherto unseen experiences for both coaches and clients. It is becoming more critical that coaches equip themselves with skills and tools that assist them to navigate not just the new normal of the mobile technologies, connectivity and virtual coaching, but the still-unknown next normal that may require new ways of coach-client interactions.

One of the most essential "master tools" for coaches to become agile, versatile and able to meet the client where they are, is to hone their interrelationship skills. Yes, you guessed it, this starts with refining the ability to greet and genuinely connect across social, cultural, ethnic, religious and the whole gamut of differences, be they assumed or real.

Humans greet to establish connection

In some cultures, people grasp your hand firmly, almost crushing it. It is regarded as good business etiquette to have a firm handshake especially for a businessperson, right?

Not really. I have encountered amazing people who offer the tips of their fingers in a limp effort to touch your hand and leave you feeling like you have just tried in vain to grasp the slippery tail of a wet fish. Yes, this is the Wet Fishtail Handshake. But if the intent behind the "quality of the handshake" is pure and genuinely positive, the Wet Fishtail Handshake may not result in a poor initial connection after all.

Yes, we are all allowed to greet the way we wish, as long as we ensure that it as a conscious greeting.

In 2016, I spent three months as a visiting professor at a university in Tokyo, and learned the Japanese art of bowing as you greet. Bowing is powerful. It says "I see you" in much the same way as the Zulu *sawubona*. I have never felt more seen, acknowledged and noticed by everyone I met as I did in Tokyo. It is what *namaste* means in many Asian communities; that the light in me recognises the light in you.

The gift or the gift wrapping

In a simplified way, choosing to greet or not greet, or to relate differently to people because of the colour of their skin or their culture and religion, is like choosing to value a gift-wrapping more than the gift itself. The gift wrapping is the superficial external stuff (like our skin). If there is anything humankind can take from the recent BlackLivesMatter movement, it must be that it is time to revisit the way we relate across these constructed superficial differences that have long been proven to be inauthentic. We will do well to seek to connect to the gift that is in every one of us.

This means starting with an intentional conscious greeting.

Greeting is inherently contextual

As the new manager or leader, your new team is like your new family. Like everyone else, your people are all energy, and they will both *sense* and *feel* you and where you are. People generally know whether you are being genuine or not. When we are inauthentic, others can feel it. This is especially true when we are working, living and relating to others closely at work and home. Many people can quite easily sense fake attempts at connection. So, it helps to simply be real. This is especially true for new teams still forming or searching for rhythm and resonance.

The conscious greeting exercise earlier in this chapter works well for new recruits seeking to connect with their new teammates, or for new leaders who aim to grow their new teams. The magical effect is in the *how* of doing the actual greeting. Critical signs of authenticity are somewhere in the body language, tone of voice, body posture or positioning, eye contact or not, and many other observable signs that the other person perceives as you engage.

The reader will note that this is vastly different – and more difficult, or far easier – depending on the socio-cultural context in which one finds themselves. Although a generalisation: it can be more difficult to attempt to carry out this basic human connection exercise in Anglo-Saxon or Western-influenced cultures and contexts in the northern hemisphere, than it is in parts of Asia, Latin America, the Caribbean and Africa.

It is important to remain in control of our own impulses and emotions, and to stay grounded. Ideally, when greeting someone we have never met before, it is important not to make it awkward or – as younger people call it – "creepy". So, how do you make that initial connection when you meet your people for the first time? Have you ever stopped to review your standard greeting? It is all about habits.

Habits take time to form and habituate. They may take even longer to undo later when they no longer serve us. With clear intent, focus and commitment, we can undo non-serving habits and replace them with new ones. The idea is to be able to connect upfront. This is why we have started with a section on greetings. You will be surprised by how powerful the exercises are in waking people up to the benefits of *"connective greetings"*.

After doing the greeting exercise, many leaders say they "wake up" to how beneficial *"intentional greeting"* is. I like to call it *"conscious greeting"*. With practice and habituation, we learn how to disconnect from people and the world around us. Eventually and gradually, we have come to normalise this "disconnection". In the process, we have lost out on the powerful connection benefits derived from "conscious greeting".

We owe it to our higher and more "woke" selves to come out of hiding from behind the corporate game of "leave me alone" and "greeting is a waste of business time". In the wake of the Fourth Industrial Revolution, we owe it to ourselves and to the rest of humanity to revisit the power of human connection. The best way to start is with a greeting. For new managers and leaders of teams, greeting is one of the best ways to lay solid foundations for building your new corporate team. Please note that these tips vary in emphasis depending on each organisational scenario or situation, and executives or managers can use some and not necessarily all of the selected tips. This practice provides an important basis for establishing genuine human connection. In the modern or virtual workplace, there is greater need for agility and adaptation of these essential practices to ensure authentic and genuine connection.

Conclusion

This chapter shared the value of the ancient philosophy of Ubuntu, and then presented the emerging and powerful concept of Ubuntu coaching as used in onboarding, socialising and coaching new (and old) leaders in new roles. Ubuntu coaching is presented in this chapter as a useful instrument for establishing rapport and genuine connection. One of the key features of the chapter is the presentation of SEEN, another useful model and tool for socialisation and onboarding.

The chapter also explored the value of "conscious greetings" to establish rapport that enables, unleashes and facilitates authentic human interconnections. The important take-away from the chapter is the practice of "conscious greeting". The awareness and alertness to the potential ramifications from an impactful greeting can help us change our first encounters into meaningful investments in long-term relationships.

Exercise: Stereotypes and assumptions about others we take as real

Here we refer to worldviews that are inherited from our upbringing, from families, from social networks, from education and culture, and from other shared perspectives. This is as opposed to rethinking, reframing and re-seeing how we look at the world from our own life experiences.

Complete the following statements as honestly as you can:

1. My top stereotypes and assumptions about others are …

2. Other people's stereotypes and assumptions about me include …

Answer the following question:

3. How can I start to see, hear and experience others as they want to be seen?

Chapter 7

Stories of Ubuntu and connection practices from senior coaches

Background

In July 2023 I was able to interview three senior, highly qualified and experienced business coaches who are all adept at applying Ubuntu concepts and principles. The following brief highlights from their extensive professional profiles merely hint at the wealth of knowledge and wisdom they bring to their work:

- *Nobantu Mpotulo* is an Ubuntu executive coach, trainer and facilitator who helps leaders "do human better" by leading with heart and backbone. Nobantu obtained a BA in Personnel Management from the University of Fort Hare, a Postgraduate Diploma in Human Resources Management from the University of Johannesburg, and an MA in Guidance and Counselling from Durham University in the UK. She has many years' experience coaching executives and teams in the private sector, government, higher education institutions and non-profit organisations. Nobantu has been able to humanise leadership through developing Ubuntu-centred leadership programmes and her Ubuntu Coach Training Programme. She was the first black African to be accredited as a Master Coach (MCC) by the International Coach Federation (ICF), and is among the 6 per cent of coaches globally with that accreditation. She is also an Enneagram teacher, a Gestalt practitioner, an NLP practitioner, a Buddhist and a mindfulness teacher, and uses Buddhist principles coupled with Ubuntu in her coaching and leadership development, which are based on the raising of consciousness and awareness. Nobantu was also a facilitator of Truth and Reconciliation Commission healing workshops for victims and perpetrators of apartheid-related violence in South Africa.

- *Dr Sharon Munyaka* is registered with the Health Professions Council of South Africa (HPCSA) as an Industrial and Organisational Psychologist. She obtained a BPsych (Hons) from Africa University in Zimbabwe, an MCom in Industrial Psychology from the University of Fort Hare, and a DCom in Industrial Psychology from Nelson Mandela University. Sharon has over 20 years' experience in transforming behaviour in the workplace for corporate clients across multiple industries, and works at an individual, team and organisational level. An experienced leadership coach and strong facilitator, Sharon is accredited in Results-Based Coaching, ORSC, LUMINA, the Enneagram and as a Theory U facilitator, and teaches coaching modules at business schools.

She is an accredited mediator with Conflict Dynamics in South Africa and the Centre for Effective Dispute Resolution in the UK. Sharon was President of the Society for Industrial and Organisational Psychology of South Africa (SIOPSA) for the 2022–2023 year, and is currently serving as Past President (2023–2024). She is the Deputy National Chairperson and serves on the board of the South African Medico-Legal Association, is a recognised expert witness on civil litigation matters in South African courts, and works on arbitration matters in the workplace. Sharon also serves on the board of Citizen Leader Lab, and supports leaders committed to transforming education in South Africa. She is a Trustee of the South African Educational Trust formed to aid Industrial and Organisational Psychology students and graduates in their careers. Regularly invited as a keynote speaker to address leadership topics at conferences and corporate events, Sharon uses her vocation for social progress.

- *Nankhonde Kasonde-van den Broek* is an executive coach and organisational change architect. She has a BA in Management from Webster University in Geneva, Switzerland; an MSc in Management from the University of Quebec in Canada; an MBA in Project Management from the African Institute of Management in Dakar, Senegal; and a joint Executive Specialised Masters in Change Leadership from HEC Paris Business School in France and Oxford University in the UK. Following a decade working in international development and finance, Nankhonde returned to Zambia to contribute to her country and the wider African development agenda. She has over 20 years' experience supporting multinationals, international organisations and governments through designing and leading large-scale change. Nankhonde has coached hundreds of clients across many organisations in Zambia and several other African countries. She is a pioneer in using technology to develop affordable and accessible coaching and human capital development solutions for Africa, built from African norms, applying her philosophy of "African cultural and context-centred design" in leadership development. Nankhonde was the first Board Chair of the Financial Sector Executive Coaching Advisory Board for Africa, now called the Africa Executive Coaching Council (based in Kenya), and a Founding Board member of the Africa Board for Coaching, Consulting and Coaching Psychology (based in South Africa). She is a Marshall Goldsmith 50 Global Leading Coach, won the coveted Thinkers50 Marshall Goldsmith Coaching and Mentoring Award in 2021, and was a Global Guru World's Top 30 Coach for 2021 and 2022. Nankhonde is a member of the Zambia Institute of Human Resource Management, and holds an Advanced Professional Diploma in Human Resource Management. She is also a member of the Chartered Institute of Arbitrators and the Institute of Directors in Zambia.

Nobantu Mpotulo

You and your roles

Q: What are your current professional roles and responsibilities, and what are your personal passions or activities?

A: One of the few blessed people doing the work I am doing at 60 years old. It is more than developing people's potential, it is taking this big heart of mine and bringing love to whoever I work with. I am so sure of what I do. People find the love, and are shocked by what they have within them. Women leaders are my niche. I help them balance the feminine and heart with their backbone and strength. How to be vulnerable and bring empathy and see amazing results. This is exactly what Ubuntu is. I help people connect to their Ubuntu brilliance. We love each other and hold each other accountable. Bring all of you to what you do. Be strong enough to be authentic and to show up with love.

Q: How would you describe yourself right now, and what informs your identity?

A: I knew when I grew up that there was something in the love I grew up with. We had rich friends materially, yet they wanted to be around us because of the love and abundance of being and heart. If a child does not feel the warmth of the village, the child will burn the village.

Q: How would you describe your past styles of leadership, and how has it transformed as we have moved into our current digital age?

A: I completed my first degree at 19. By that age I was a career guidance professional at a university in the 1980s; this helped me grow as a leader. Most of the students were older than me. I sometimes meet some of those former students, and they tell me that I helped shape them and their leadership through love and connection at the same time. I recall being assisted by the Vice-Chancellor to go and do my Masters degree at Durham University in the UK after a year (instead of five years after appointment); they broke the rules for me. The university supported my development; I still got paid while on scholarship.

Q: In your leadership journey what barriers have you encountered along the way, and how did you overcome them?

A: At the university I was a counsellor, and I got asked to act as Director. I was leading people who were older than me. People questioned why this young woman was acting Director. But I did not douse others' flames, I helped them shine. Soon after that (after 10 years), I left and became a Director for Counselling services, my first role as an executive. Vice-Chancellor Mzamane used to call me and have coffee chats with me to get my views on leadership issues. What was amazing was how elders identified the wisdom early on and still approached me. It was never about age. I became an elder from a very young age.

Q: Describe situations where you had to unlearn or let go of attachments or even had identity loss?

A: During my sixtieth birthday recently, people mentioned that I am a pusher. They say that I get things done: 'If you want to get things done, get Nobantu onto it.' I have passion and fire, and this is the time when I lose a bit of the heart identity that I hold dear in my way of leading. I can push people beyond limits, and know that things can unfold. As Victor Frankl said, 'Between stimulus and response there is a space. In that space is our power to choose our response. In our response lies our growth and freedom.' This is the motto I live by. Pause. Pause. Pause.

Q: Describe an incident where you were effective as a leader: what did you change and what did you learn?

A: When I was working at Telkom in 1999 as Study Skills Development Manager, managing a budget of over R100 million, I helped get children who were good in science, technology, engineering and mathematics (STEM) subjects, and assisted them. I changed the policy and made it accessible. I recognised the gems in everyone and polished them.

Q: Describe an incident where you were ineffective as a leader: what did you change, and what did you learn?

A: My passion can override things, e.g. in over-convincing others, how to bring things together, and making sure that everything works.

Ubuntu and its role

Q: How has Ubuntu played a role in your professional and/or personal life, and how has it shaped you as a leader?

A: When I was given an opportunity as an ethical coach, and to work with diverse people, I saw how they are able to see the goodness in themselves and get in touch with themselves and their higher selves. People thank me for touching their lives and for changing the world. They know my heart.

Q: How do Ubuntu and human connection skills assist you in reaching or achieving your aspirations?

A: See more. Hear more. Love more. Illuminate more. Be more for others to become, and light the whole world. This is what I have done and am doing. People are bringing that to me, and they are opening to loving more.

Q: How does Ubuntu and connection impact you in all of your relationships?

A: My grandchildren say I am the greatest *MaKhulu* (grandma). They say love is in my eyes.

Q: How can Ubuntu support organisations in onboarding new employees or leaders?

A: I was in a session with Marshall Goldsmith and others, and we worked on how people can balance leading with empathy, assertiveness and confidence. When I do that, people start to understand what is needed in each moment.

Q: How can Ubuntu support young leader-managers to become transformational change-makers in education, business and society?

A: If you want to go fast, go alone; trusting and knowing that things happen through the heart and through others. This is what takes us home to the outcomes we desire.

Q: How does Ubuntu play out in gender dynamics within organisations and in society at large?

A: I have been so fortunate to work with large financial institutions in SA, balancing the feminine and the masculine. Women need to embrace and dance with their femininity, find the balance and be non-binary. We can be whatever we need to be, and know that all the energies are accessible.

Q: What Ubuntu-related tips would you offer leaders – and particularly women and youth?

A: Knowing that with artificial intelligence (AI) and the digital age, we are being connected. When is it to be ethical with AI? It's about engaging with it with heart. What is the heartbeat of AI? How can we humanise AI and use it to impact humanity better? With heart.[82]

Dr Sharon Munyaka

You and your roles

Q: What are your current professional roles and responsibilities, and what are your personal passions or activities?

A: Currently, my role is President of SIOPSA during the 2022–2023 term; from 1 August 2023 I become Past President. I am also a Work Psychologist registered with the Health Professions Council of SA and working at an Individual, team and organisational level.

Q: How would you describe yourself right now, and what informs your identity?

A: I am human, a mother, I am a daughter, I am a sister, I am a lover, I am a friend, I am an African. I am a 'rainmaker', human connector, drawn to situations that call for courage, curiosity and compassion. Family shapes who I am and how I show up in the world. Family is much bigger than just biology. I am shaped by the desire for a world that works well and caters for all its people.

Q: How would you describe your past style of leadership, and how has it transformed as we have moved into our current digital age?

A: My default leadership style has been collaborative, although this tends to evolve based on the context. There are moments where I have had to be directive, especially where time is short and quick decision making is required. I use coaching as a style to help teams move forward. Over time, I have moved towards consultative styles where we co-create the tasks and people go away and execute independently. With hybrid work, it has redirected to one where I check-in regularly and create spaces in the day to check-in on task requirements, idea generation, and questions. Ultimately, there has been a need to create community, collaborate on projects, and allow spaciousness with deadlines and structure. As a leader, I've learnt to listen until it hurts. I don't defend my position. I listen, I pause, I reflect, and then respond. As I get older, the pressure to 'react' has diminished.

Q: In your leadership journey, what barriers have you encountered along the way, and how did you overcome them?

A: As a big-picture thinker, I found that my ideas were concrete in my head, but would not always be clear for the people I am leading. I am not scared of big ideas. Often, I would be ten steps ahead and moving to action, which did result in leaving others behind. As I grew in my leadership roles, I realised I needed to slow down, balance my enthusiasm and pace, and allow enough time for people to make sense of the ideas and formulate a structure that makes sense. The more we spend time in co-creating the plan of action, the more tasks are done well and everyone feels they have contributed. I am learning how to do the dance with big ideas and to be OK letting ideas go – if not bought – and explore others. I have learnt not to be attached. I am in the season of legacy leadership. This is bigger than me as an individual. It is about all of us, and speaks to Ubuntu and the value of the collective, the greater good, and of our common humanity. This is at the heart of Ubuntu.

Q: Describe situations where you had to unlearn or let go of attachments, or even had identity loss.

A: In my role as President of SIOPSA, I had to let go of the need to be right. I learnt that my capacity to listen to different stakeholders without defending my position allowed for more voices to be part of the conversation. I had to let go of what I wanted as an individual, and think about the broader professional body. I had to let go of me as Sharon, and rather step into a role of being a black woman at the helm of a professional body that had been historically male and white. It was quite a shift, and had its own challenges, making me approach the various issues I was confronted with differently.

Q: Describe an incident where you were effective as a leader: what did you change, and what did you learn?

A: The accrediting body for psychologists in South Africa is the Health Professions Council of South Africa (HPCSA). There is a proposed framework that was put forward, and members of the HPCSA needed to comment. Fielding the panicked calls and messages from psychologists at different stages of their career, I used my role as President of SIOPSA to lobby and advocate for industrial psychologists to have a collective voice. By engaging the community of industrial psychologists in South Africa, we managed to gather the various viewpoints and share these with the HPCSA. I learned that in every situation, the leader needs to be courageous enough to step into roles that might be unpopular, to be bold enough to speak on behalf of the masses, and to not be afraid to take on the role of a leader as required. It is about service for and to the greater good.

Q: Describe an incident where you were ineffective as a leader: what did you change, and what did you learn?

A: When I let the pressure of work get to me, I am ineffective because the work piles up, my focus shifts to delivery, and my ability to communicate effectively is reduced. I get stuck in doing several steps in my head, get frustrated when others around me don't get where I am going, and I get impatient. I have learnt that getting frustrated is not helpful. Most of the work I need to do is dependent on the input of others. I have had to be intentional about pausing, breathing, and checking-in with my team so I don't leave anyone behind.

Ubuntu and its role

Q: How has Ubuntu played a role in your professional and/or personal life – and how has it shaped you as a leader?

A: For me, Ubuntu is about my wellbeing and being intrinsically tied into the wellbeing of another person. 'When it rains, it doesn't rain only in my yard, it rains for my neighbour too.' Understanding this principle has helped me operate from a place of understanding that working in unison with others gets us much further. Together, we are whole, and therefore greater than the sum of our parts. Recognising that Ubuntu connects us beyond the individual means that we know within us that our wellbeing is tied up in others' wellbeing.

Q: How do Ubuntu and connection impact you in all of your relationships? How do Ubuntu and human connection skills assist you in reaching or achieving your aspirations?

A: I believe that the essence of Ubuntu is rooted in community, and in service to humanity. It entails the ability of an individual to express reciprocal compassion, harmony, dignity, and humanity. Ubuntu directly links with the idea that human value is not realised because an individual is dignified or worthy, but rather that they are part of humanity. This is how I live and lead in my life. This directly links to the concept of every individual possessing rights, precisely because they are human. This right is cross-culturally justified in the African, Islamic, Western, and Confucian schools of thought. We are in this life together as fellow humans, and must seek to 'see' each other and work together in all spheres of life.

Q: How can Ubuntu support organisations in onboarding new employees or leaders?

A: The use of Ubuntu as a foundational moral principle for all relationships, in the current age of the Fourth Industrial Revolution, and as the metamorphosis into the Fifth Industrial Revolution unfolds. Ubuntu can serve as a moral compass in creating and maintaining a humane workplace, which will enable sustainable and ethical products, services, and behaviour.

Q: How can Ubuntu support young leader-managers to become transformational change-makers in education, business and society?

A: Using Ubuntu as the core moral principle in creating and maintaining a humane workplace, signifies that individual and organisational actions ought to acknowledge, appreciate, and promote, human dignity and inclusion. Such inclusion should extend beyond the typical diversity-based categories of race, gender and age, to include all human beings, who are deemed to have value simply because they are human.

Q: How does Ubuntu play out in gender dynamics within organisations and in society at large?

A: Ubuntu suggests that we move beyond the individual and work as a collective. This enables more inclusion and allows society to function better and yield more.

Q: What Ubuntu-related tips would you offer leaders – and particularly women and youth?

A: Ubuntu centres around an acknowledgement of individuals becoming more self-aware, by getting to knowing others in more meaningful ways. Ubuntu is not just for me or you. It is for all of us. It is a 'life-force' and energy that propels us towards greater genuine and authentic connection and to embrace the values of humanness. It is the ultimate human ecosystem that connects all of us through all our systems.[83]

Nankhonde Kasonde-van den Broek

You and your roles

Q: Please tell us about yourself: what are some of the highlights of your life that you would like to share?

A: I am an avid philosopher, with a curiosity about co-creating success in life experiences that align with who you are. I think this comes from my experiences growing up in Zambia, Europe and then being attracted to work that gave me global experiences. My environment was constantly changing – in one year I would live within three different worldviews – so I had to find ways to identify within the reference points that built up my person and preferences.

Q: What nourishes you the most in current roles and responsibilities? What do you enjoy the most?

A: I love to watch people thrive in what they chose to do (as long as it is legal). My current roles and responsibilities give me a front-row seat into people's lives; their greatest hopes, aspirations, regrets and perspectives. In addition, I carry an awesome vantage point through my eyes into the rest of the world. This comes from the global stages that have opened doors for me to share, intentionally and strategically, my Africa. An Africa I love to protect, and at times hold accountable.

Q: How would you describe yourself right now, and what informs your identity?

A: I am a visionary. My name (*ka sonde*) means 'small earth', and I feel it in this season. My identity is informed by a continuous invitation from my heart, and an articulation in my head, for action with my feet to always push frontiers – my own and those constructed by others. The worst thing to say to me is why I can't do something, because it engages a switch in my head that will do it.

Q: How would you describe your style of leadership, and how does it play out in the digital age?

A: My style of leadership has evolved over time. I have always been an aspirational servant leader, but in reality I have had to truly grow into what it means and what it doesn't mean. I like to be in control, and balancing this has meant learning constantly how to communicate better with others so that my words no longer have to present my intent when I get it wrong; but rather, my actions now beautifully speak my soft power. I am currently leading a remote team, and this has given me the stage to really apply all levels of listening skills. Sharing a vision and creating a culture, when you are not physically present for people to receive your energy, requires skills. While I am embracing the digital age, I am very conscious of my own need to change and be open to achieving the same impact for my team and clients through the exploration of different channels.

Q: Along your leadership journey, what has enabled you to achieve your goals?

A: Mad obsession has helped me achieve my goals. I get obsessed when I see something. There is no half-in or half-out with me. Once I am in, my whole being is engaged. If it means I need to study something, I will do it; if it means I need to find a person who is doing it and learn from them, I will do it. This has also proved to be a weakness, because those around me suffer. They suffer if I don't have the skills to support their needs and their dreams. In order to better manage my relationships, I have learnt to let go and say no sometimes, because it's not what I need in that moment that matters, but what the true essence of the relationship needs. I have trusted and partnered with God on outcomes that went against what I thought, and He has shown me, when I take time to listen, why it was the right thing to do or not to do.

Q: Describe situations where you had to unlearn things or transform yourself in order to succeed.

A: When I returned home after many years of being abroad, I had to unlearn what I thought home was and what I was ready for. I have always said that coming home was the hardest transition for me, until I connected with a part of me that dismantled who I had become and reconstructed a piece of me that gave me permission to be. This became so important when my father passed away. I don't think anything else in life has ever broken me like that. I became what we call in my language *na nkoko*, a manifestation of a meaning that is embedded in my name Nankhonde, 'mother of many'. I took on roles that I did not know I had the capacity to take on. I led in ways that required strength and wisdom beyond my years and my social and traditional leanings.

Q: Think of a situation where you were effective as a leader: what led to that, what did you do?

A: I can remember a time when I took on a client engagement to support a leadership programme that was to be rolled out nationally. The project involved working with multiple stakeholders with different agendas; and as a member of the coordinating project team, I found myself propelled into organisational politics that tested my ability to effectively navigate and facilitate different perspectives, powers and levels of integrity. I like to think that I came out on the right side of history because I am at peace. During this period, I had to stand up for what I felt was right, but also had to respect others in the process. I had to negotiate with soft and sometimes hard power, and know which was needed when. This project stressed me, and it lasted over a period of two years.

Ubuntu and its role

Q: Think of a situation where you were ineffective as a leader: what led to that, and what did you learn?

A: I can no longer count the number of times I have failed in life, but I can remember the deep imprint of transformation that the failure was always already implying. I remember when my commitments exceeded my capacity to deliver. I recently heard an interesting quote, that it is not a lack of time that constrains us but rather a lack of focus. I am ineffective when I don't say no. This is something I am still working on, and in the last five years it has really taken its toll in some of my relationships. The wisdom comes in knowing that even if I want to or can do something, the world will not end if I don't. When I am not operating at that level of consciousness, the reality for myself and others is sad.

Q: What does the practice and concept of Ubuntu mean to you in the digital, hybrid and/or virtual world?

A: I see Ubuntu as a way of being, a new experience and manifestation of what the digital age is inviting us to co-create. At its core it is an energy, so in its very essence it is not something tangible. I think that Ubuntu remains a spirit that can be invoked and revoked by our actions. What the digital age has done is provide us with a floodgate of tools that appear to facilitate its expression in the magnitude of relationships to which we now have physical and virtual access; but in that very magnitude is solitude. It's the solitude that we need to work on. A form of solitude that starts with self and is then complemented by others. If the self is not a piece, then the other cannot connect. The digital age has not changed that principle; if anything, it has made it even more important as we get into the age of metaverses and virtual lives, friends, neighbourhoods. These are all just longings for something that does not exist within.

Q: How does Ubuntu as a way of being show up in your relationships, and especially in how you lead?

A: For me, Ubuntu is a way of life. It is my culture; it is my reference point for who I am and what I need and am nourished by. In my business, Ubuntu is one of the five values. As a founder, my team knows that my success is their success, and as they support the achievement of my dream, I am actively feeding theirs. In my family and relationships, we are a clan. What vibrates at one end is felt at the other end. We co-exist.

Q: How does Ubuntu or human connection assist you towards reaching or achieving your biggest goals?

A: Ubuntu gives back to me what I give it; it's like a boomerang. My biggest goals have been met because I gave and received from others in equal measure (and sometimes cumulative disproportionate measure) the blessings of my forefathers. I am reaping the blessings and prayers of generations. I don't think it, I know it; God has told me several times as the boomerang was landing. This energy transcends time and place.

Q: What can Ubuntu or human connection do to support organisations in onboarding new employees?

A: Ubuntu is a beautiful concept, but to truly understand it you must understand true relationships. Often, we speak about the power of being emotionally and socially intelligent. What that is, is an ability to exist and vibrate in relationships and strengthen them like three strings when there is discord and when there is not. The true essence of Ubuntu is an ability to really see deeply into yourself and others. To work through within, in each season, your own limitations, frustrations and hold them reverently sometimes in silence, sometimes in loud expression. It is a response, a dance, a challenge and an opportunity that lives daily in all our interactions. Organisations tend to provide technical and operational onboarding; we don't provide human onboarding and relationship systems onboarding.

Q: What role can Ubuntu play in supporting youth to be transformational leaders in a changing world?

A: You cannot reap capacity that you have not built. It is as much a reflection of the teacher as it is the student. Plain and simple, teach them how to connect with themselves and connect with others. To see discord as information that can inform accord. I believe in relationship systems, and that the system is naturally creative, resourceful and whole. That what happens in a system is not by accident, and that it also knows what I need. This generation of youth in Africa is a mega-system. We created it. They will transform it. You cannot deal with a problem at the same level you created it. Raising this generation of youth through individual and collective parenting of brokenness and healing alongside segregation, poverty, disease and war is showing. And it's OK. It's a different energy that they will speak to, that they will co-parent individually and collectively to inclusion, prosperity, health and peace.

Q: How does Ubuntu play out in gender dynamics within organisations with respect to the digital age?

A: Unhealthy organisations show symptoms of disease in different ways. When there is a deficiency there is a need to supplement. The state of women in society is mirrored in organisational experience. The digital age has made more visible practices and behaviours that previously remained hidden. With access to information, knowledge is democratised and people are connected. In the digital age activism has been propelled to a level of potential impact that previously was reserved for limited causes. Organisations are becoming more human. COVID-19 taught us many things. It showed us that we can work and live differently if we have to. I think one of my biggest observations of COVID is what it did to women and their relationship with work. Many women caught up on years' worth of certain hours of home life that had previously been impossible for them to experience. For some this was positive, although for others we saw the continued stain of gender-based violence during a time where there were limited or no safe havens to run to. What COVID-19 did is force a change in conditions that women in organisations have been advocating. The digital age has made it possible for organisations to know that they can function designed around what is most effective and most healthy for humans, rather than the other way around. I think we will continue to see the organisations of the future designed for people in the way they serve their customers and host their employees. This will take Ubuntu to co-create what works best for all of us, because the constructs of night and day, working hours and non-working hours became blurred during COVID. I heard an interesting reference recently which questioned work–life balance, and affirmed that if we had only life, and work was just one part of its puzzle, then we would shape and do things that would suit living a fulfilled and healthy life experience mentally, emotionally and physically.

Q: What are your views on Ubuntu, gender, and leadership in the digital world?

A: They are all evolving at different paces, and will be misaligned as a result. The key is to know where each one is at any given point in time in history and its purpose. Ubuntu is both the glue and the fuel.

Q: Without Ubuntu, our youth are lost, and humanity's future is doomed. What do you think of this?

A: Where is Ubuntu going? I do not think we are lost. Systems are dynamic. I think we are not recognising the season that needs to come to pass and will pass.

Q: What Ubuntu-related tips would you offer leaders who want to grow other leaders in the digital age?

A: Relationships matter. As a leader, I am aware that I must distribute my leadership and let it be felt.[84]

Exercise: Ubuntu in your life

Do this exercise with a partner.

1. Describe how you have experienced Ubuntu in your life.

2. Think about a leader whose Ubuntu qualities you have experienced at first hand, and share what you have learned from them as a result.

Conclusion

This chapter shared the perspectives of three senior coaches on Ubuntu in coaching, in leadership, and in life in general. A critical perspective and indirect message in their sharing is that Ubuntu management and Ubuntu coaching have a vital role to play in sharpening leader-managers as they enter new organisational systems.

Chapter 8

Self-reflection for leader-managers

This chapter is an exercise in its own right.

One of the best questions we can ask ourselves is "Who am I?" When the answers to this question come from deep within our souls, the magical powers of self-awareness start working.

This chapter focuses on tools, tips and instruments that new leader-managers and recruits can use to self-reflect and deepen their self-awareness in their new roles. This is especially important for leader-managers and their teams in fast-changing business environments in the new and increasingly hybrid world of work.

Introducing the seven Self-Reflection Questions

For over 12 years, one of the reliable leadership self-discovery tools I have used to get to know some of my coaching clients better, and to help them know themselves even better, has been the seven Self-Reflection Questions (SRQs). The SRQs have been a dependable instrument while working with onboarding clients, especially new leader-managers seeking to tap into their inherent strengths to show up the best way they can with their new teams.

The development of these SRQs has been based on the value drawn from repeated use and their perceived relevance as expressed by numerous clients. Most of their usability and relevance is drawn from experience with executive clients across multiple sectors who have shared anecdotal evidence that working with the SRQs helped them see many blind spots that they were not aware they had. Some have shared that responding to the SRQs in their own time was like holding up a mirror to themselves, and they could then see themselves clearly. The SRQs are powerful as an awareness instrument, especially when working with leadership clients who want to develop their leadership skills and have an interest in sharpening their self-awareness.

The SRQs are a versatile tool that can present as a combination of probing and reflective questions meant to support deeper introspection by whomever is working with them. In my leadership skills development work, I use the SRQs at the start of the leadership engagement journey with a client.

The SRQs do not work with every client in the moment. Some clients take the questions away and answer each question in their own time. Then they reflect on their responses to each question in one-to-one engagement sessions. In most situations, the SRQs work well as triggers of personal reflections which deepen self-awareness, and sometimes help leaders change direction or refine their leadership repertoire.

Responses to the seven SRQs have ranged from surprising one-liners or one sentence per question, through multiple pages per question, all the way to multimedia PowerPoint presentations with beautifully-crafted slides featuring photographs and video clips. The SRQs are drawn from multiple sources, including other reflection instruments that I have come across during 25 years' experience as a coach, leadership skills development facilitator and human development practitioner.

Self-Reflection Question 1: Who am I?

SRQ 1 looks and sounds like a simple and straightforward question to answer. Yet it can easily become a trick question. Often, when they start responding to SRQ 1, leadership clients tend to pause momentarily and then suddenly exclaim something to the effect that this is a challenging question. Clients sometimes give long descriptions of who they believe they are, based on previous personality or other assessments. Some share feedback given by their clients, managers, peers and direct reports.

When answering this question, it helps if you do not focus on the given roles that you play in your job or at home. Ideally, the recommendation here is to go deeper into what you believe defines you. Better still, you can respond by describing what you stand for and who you are, if and when all other given roles are taken away. Suddenly it becomes less of a simple question and more of a deeper issue, igniting profound insights and sharpening self-awareness. At the start of a new role in a new organisational system and with a new team, this can be powerful for a new recruit to work with.

Self-Reflection Question 2: Where am I?

SRQ 2 helps clients check where they are in their life-journey, or how far they are towards achieving their desired objectives or living their life purpose or vision. It is not about geographical location.

Sometimes it helps for clients to draw a lifeline or timeline of their lives, dating back from when they were born, through the first day at school, all the way up to the present. Clients tend to respond to this question by reflecting on their achievements such as educational qualifications, graduations, employment and promotions. Others respond by referring to marital status, and/or having children; or by referring to what is expected of them by their families, including buying property, paying off student debt, or becoming financially independent. It is quite useful to think about it in all areas of your life: personal, social, educational and professional, including significant relationships through each decade of your life. A final tip here is to draw up your life plan and measure your progress against it.

Self-Reflection Question 3: Where am I going?

SRQ 3 is sometimes referred to as the anchor question. This label came from some clients who suggested that responding to this question made them feel anchored and grounded. One of the lessons from working with this question is the powerfully reflective and emotional states that multiple clients experience when they ask themselves where they are going. The journey metaphor tends to ignite deeper reflection on life as a continuous journey with ups and downs, and with multiple crossroads.

This question has also been referred to as the vision question, or purpose-driven reflective question. It helps for clients to ask themselves the question, "What is the vision and purpose for my life and/or my career?", or "What is my vision and purpose for this team?"

Self-Reflection Question 4: How will I know I have arrived where I am going?

SRQ 4 addresses the issue of measurement of progress towards set goals and targets. It is not just a check on achievement or lack thereof. Responses here include graduation, training courses attended, marriage, children and promotions. This is a tracking question that demands solid responses or tangible achievements.

To help clients or team members during reflection, using this question implies that they had a plan against whose implementation they are checking their progress. This is where the coach or the leader can see the interconnections of the questions and responses from the different SRQs.

Self-Reflection Question 5: What are my life's major landmarks along my journey?

SRQ 5 takes responses to SRQ 4 to the next level. Sometimes SRQ 4 and SRQ 5 are combined to help give a comprehensive response.

One useful tip to use in helping your team members or clients reflect on SRQ 5 is to check what their life goals are, and to refer to their earlier responses in all four SRQs before this one.

Self-Reflection Question 6: What is my support system?

SRQ 6 is one of the most powerful self-reflection questions, that in particular helps new leader-managers and other clients entering new organisational systems become aware of who or what they can rely on for support. Responses here may include spouses, family, friends, meditation, prayer, mindfulness, reading, gardening, hiking, physical exercise and travelling abroad.

One of the most useful approaches in working with this SRQ is to briefly share your own support system as a leader or coach. As an avid gardener myself, I have found that sharing this with a client often helps them feel safe enough to share some of their rather unusual support systems. This involves the concept of self that we use as Gestalt practitioners, and it can be powerful for creating psychological safety. It is a very personal piece of reflection, and demands respect and understanding.

Important: Please do not laugh if the team member or client shared what to you appears to be a seemingly "weird" support system or activity. Simply acknowledge it.

Self-Reflection Question 7: What is my service to humanity in our interconnected world?

SRQ 7 is a legacy question that seeks to find out about our own, our team members' or clients' greater collective impact and service to humanity. It is the ultimate Ubuntu question about service to the greater good and to humanity, beyond the narrow self-service of many individuals across many diverse societies.

One recommended way to help team members or clients reflect deeply on this is to heighten their awareness of the greater role their organisational system plays. Alternatively, coaches or facilitators working with clients on this can ask about "insertion points", or areas of intervention that they can make or have made with success, and then check where they believe they can still make a difference.

Additional self-reflection tools for new leader-managers

In some of my team coaching and leadership skills development sessions, I have asked many team leaders or leader-managers to ask themselves the following two questions:

- Do people really feel safe enough to always be honest with me, or to be truly themselves in their full integrity around me?

- How do people change when they are around me?

These reflection tools can become your best instruments for discovering what makes your new team tick. Most businesses have rules, procedures, guidelines and values that govern employees' behaviour. Beyond the above questions and the seven SRQs, I have also found the following bonus questions useful for establishing integrity and respect by new leader-managers right from Day One at work:

- What is the core business strategy?

- What is the organisational or team culture?

- What is the shadow culture? What existing patterns and behaviours need to be stopped now?

- What are the team's values?

- What are the informal rules and values?

- Who are the opinion-makers? Who are the informal leaders, coaches and mentors?

- Who are the "workplace parents"?

- Who are the "office children"?

- What are the possible blind sides for leaders in this role?

- What new things do I need to introduce or do differently?

- What exemplary behaviours or patterns must I start modelling (e.g. arrive earlier at work)?

Conclusion

These SRQs have served me well over the years. They can provide valuable reflection data for both new leader-managers and their teams, so that both parties start seeing each other clearly as they show up, and do not rely on hearsay or one-sided stories about each other. I hope they can support you on your journey with others. For new leader-managers reading this, feel free to use these tools with new teams you are building.

Exercise: Reflections on what you will change from reading this book

My reflections:

_____

_____

_____

_____

_____

_____

_____

_____

_____

_____

_____

_____

_____

_____

_____

_____

_____

_____

_____

_____

_____

_____

_____

_____

_____

_____

_____

_____

_____

_____

Chapter 9

In conclusion

The first book in the *Management Mastery and Practice Series* edited by Dr Sunny Stout-Rostron is titled *Everything You Ever Wanted To Know About Managing People But Were Afraid To Ask*. Among other great resources therein, the book introduced the reader to a comprehensive body of core principles for managing people in the modern workplace.

This, the second book in the series is about *Ubuntu Coaching and Connection Practices for Leader-Managers*. It takes a step further beyond self-mastery and managing people, and delves into practical tools and techniques to support leader-managers as they venture into their new management and leadership roles. I hope that this book has provided practical suggestions for human connection to assist in navigating workplace relationships.

Our entry into new workplaces can set us up for success quicker and more effectively when we master the ability to establish genuine and authentic connections with those we encounter during the early entry period. The process of onboarding and socialising new leader-managers is not only the responsibility of human capital officials in the workplace. When onboarding is everyone's responsibility, and when there is a genuine culture of engagement, with Ubuntu intelligence, dynamic transformational cultures can be established across any shared spaces.

The book shared tools and techniques for establishing meaningful human relationships, starting with conscious and intentional connection with others wherever we encounter them. It highlighted that when we greet consciously, mindfully and intentionally, we co-create and establish genuine and authentic connections that may lead to life-long relationships.

In the unpredictable, fast-paced change directly impacting workplace relationships, powered by the relentless introduction of new mobile technologies and artificial intelligence, new leader-managers need all the assistance they can get to connect with their new teams. This book presented and shared human connection tools and practices that anyone can access and utilise to find their feet swiftly at work and build strong rapport and resonance.

With the practical illustrative examples in the book, and the tips and tools at the end of every chapter, this book can be a ready companion for leader-managers and other new hires who need agility and speed to adapt to their new organisational environments.

The new leader-manager whose task is to build a high-performing and value-adding team in increasingly complex shared spaces stands a better chance of success when they deploy the Ubuntu connection tools shared in this book. Our hope is that you can also utilise heart-sets and Ubuntu intelligence.

Bibliography

De Liefde, W. (2011). *Lekgotla: The art of leadership through dialogue*. Second edition. Johannesburg: Jacana.

Drucker, P.F. (2005). Managing oneself. (Reprint of article published in 1999.) *Harvard Business Review*, 10:2–14.

Du Toit, C. (2019). *Onboarding: Strategies for getting employees up to speed faster*. Randburg: Knowres.

Duhigg, C. (2016). *Smarter Faster Better: The secrets of being productive in life and business*. New York, NY: Random House.

Gafni, M. (2001). *Soul Prints: Your path to fulfilment*. New York, NY: Simon & Schuster.

Global Team Coaching Institute (GTCI) (2021). *Gateway to Team Coaching Program: Module 1: Teams and Teaming*. Global Team Coaching Institute, in collaboration with WBECS.

Goleman, D. (1996). *Emotional Intelligence: Why it can matter more than IQ*. London: Bloomsbury.

Goleman, D. (2006). *Social Intelligence: The new science of human relationships*. London: Hutchinson.

Goleman, D., Boyatzis, R., and McKee, A. (2001). Primal Leadership: The hidden driver of great performance. *Harvard Business Review*, December, 79(11): 42–51.

Goleman, D., Boyatzis, R., and McKee, A. (2002a). *Primal Leadership: Realizing the power of emotional intelligence*. Boston, MA: Harvard Business Review Press.

Goleman, D., Boyatzis, R., and McKee, A. (2002b). *The New Leaders: Transforming the art of leadership into the science of results*. London: Time/Warner.

Hamel, G., and Breen, B. (2007). *The Future of Management*. Boston, MA: Harvard Business School Press.

Hanafin, J. (2004). Rules of thumb for awareness agents: With a tip o' the hat to Herb Shepard. *OD Practitioner*, 36(4):24–28.

Kasonde-van den Broek, N. (2023). Personal interview. Johannesburg, 18 July.

Khoza, R.J. (2011). *Attuned Leadership: African humanism as compass*. Johannesburg: Penguin.

Kline, N. (1999). *Time To Think: Listening to ignite the human mind*. London: Cassell.

Kline, N. (2021). The Ten Components of a Thinking Environment, Worksheet, 2023.

Magadlela, D. (2008). (Mis)understanding ubuntu: A reply. *Mail & Guardian Thought Leader*, 16 March. URL: thoughtleader.co.za/mis-understanding-ubuntu-a-reply/.

Magadlela, D. (2015). The 'P' stance for leaders in meetings. *Business Essentials*, 10 September. URL: www.businessessentials.co.za/2015/09/10/the-p-stance-for-leaders-in-meetings/.

Magadlela, D. (2019). The case for Ubuntu Coaching: Working with an African coaching meta-model that strengthens human connection in a fast-changing VUCA world. In Stout-Rostron, S. (ed.), *Transformational Coaching to Lead Culturally Diverse Teams* (pp. 85–101). Abingdon, Oxon: Routledge.

Magadlela, D. (2020). Sawubona – "I see you": The understated power of greeting in coaching and human relationships. *COACH Magazine*, 31 August. URL: www.coach-magazine. com/sawubona-i-see-you/.

Makho (2019). Personal interview. Johannesburg, 7 September.

MindTools (2021). *Virtual Onboarding: How to Get Your New Hire on Board – Online*. MindTools. com. URL: www.mindtools.com/pages/article/virtual-onboarding.htm. Accessed 14 February 2021.

Mpotulo, N. (2023). Personal interview. Johannesburg, 6 July.

Msila, V. (2015). *Ubuntu: Shaping the current workplace with (African) wisdom*. Randburg: Knowres.

Munyaka, S. (2023) Personal interview. Johannesburg, 5 July.

Nobantu Coaching (2021). *Ubuntu Coaching for Coaches*. Training session dates: 6, 13, 20 and 27 March 2021. URL: nobantucoaching.co.za/services/.

Nussbaum, B., Palsule, S., and Mkhize, V. (2010). *Personal Growth African Style*. Johannesburg: Penguin.

Pampallis, P. (2011). *The Coaching Centre Newsletter*, 14 October.

Pampallis, P. (2021). *Urban Hub 23 – Integral Africa: Thriveable Cities*. Cape Town: IntegralMentors.

Parker, M. (2014). *It's Not What you Say, It's How you Say It!* London: Random House.

Penteado, C. (2017). Welcome to the VUCA world! *The People Side*, 26 September. URL: www. thepeopleside.com/blog/what-the-heck-is-vuca.

Rød, A., and Fridjhon, M. (2016). *Creating Intelligent Teams: Leading with Relationship Systems Intelligence*. Johannesburg: Knowres.

Rosinski, P. (2003). *Coaching Across Cultures: New tools for leveraging national, corporate and professional differences*. London: Nicholas Brealey.

Rukuni, M. (2009). *Leading Afrika*. Johannesburg: Penguin.

Schwab, K., and Davis, N. (2018). *Shaping the Future of the Fourth Industrial Revolution*. New York, NY: Currency.

Sridharan, M. (2021). *BANI – How To Make Sense Of A Chaotic World?* Think Insights, 29 July. URL: thinkinsights.net/leadership/bani/.

Stout-Rostron, S. (2019). Theories, models and tools informing the High-Performance Relationship Coaching Model. In Stout-Rostron, S. (ed.), *Transformational Coaching to Lead Culturally Diverse Teams* (pp. 44–73). Abingdon, Oxon: Routledge.

Tutu, D. (1995). Nothing short of a miracle. In Thick, C. (ed.), *The Right To Hope: Global problems, global visions: Creative responses to our world in need* (pp. 1–4). London: Earthscan.

Wilber, K., Patten, T., Leonard, A., and Morelli, M. (2008). *Integral Life Practice: A 21st-century blueprint for physical health, emotional balance, mental clarity, and spiritual awakening*. Boston, MA: Shambhala.

Endnotes

1   Goleman, D. (1996). *Emotional Intelligence: Why it can matter more than IQ.* London: Bloomsbury.

2   Goleman, D., Boyatzis, R., and McKee, A. (2002a). *Primal Leadership: Realizing the power of emotional intelligence.* Boston, MA: Harvard Business Review Press.

3   Goleman, D., Boyatzis, R., and McKee, A. (2002b). *The New Leaders: Transforming the art of leadership into the science of results.* London: Time/Warner.

4   Kline, N. (1999). *Time To Think: Listening to ignite the human mind.* London: Cassell.

5   Goleman, D. (2006). *Social Intelligence: The new science of human relationships.* London: Hutchinson.

6   Rukuni, M. (2009). *Leading Afrika.* Johannesburg: Penguin, p156.

7   Stout-Rostron, S. (2022). *Everything You Ever Wanted To Know About Managing People But Were Afraid to Ask.* Randburg: KR Publishing.

8   Wilber, K., Patten, T., Leonard, A., and Morelli, M. (2008). *Integral Life Practice: A 21st-century blueprint for physical health, emotional balance, mental clarity, and spiritual awakening.* Boston, MA: Shambhala.

9   Ibid, p9.

10 Ibid.

11 Pampallis, P. (2011). *The Coaching Centre Newsletter,* 14 October.

12 Hanafin, J. (2004). Rules of thumb for awareness agents: With a tip o' the hat to Herb Shepard. *OD Practitioner,* 36(4):24–28.

13 Sridharan, M. (2021). *BANI – How To Make Sense Of A Chaotic World?* Think Insights, 29 July. URL: thinkinsights.net/leadership/bani/.

14 Penteado, C. (2017). Welcome to the VUCA world! *The People Side,* 26 September. URL: www.thepeopleside.com/blog/what-the-heck-is-vuca.

15 Ibid, p2.

16 Sridharan, 2021.

17 Ibid.

18 Ibid.

19 Global Team Coaching Institute (GTCI) (2021). *Gateway to Team Coaching Program: Module 1: Teams and Teaming.* Global Team Coaching Institute, in collaboration with WBECS.

20 Duhigg, C. (2016). *Smarter Faster Better: The secrets of being productive in life and business.* New York, NY: Random House.

21 MindTools (2021). *Virtual Onboarding: How to Get Your New Hire on Board – Online.* MindTools.com. URL: www.mindtools.com/pages/article/virtual-onboarding.htm. Accessed 14 February 2021, p1.

22 Du Toit, C. (2019). *Onboarding: Strategies for getting employees up to speed faster.* Randburg: KR Publishing.

23 Ibid.

24 De Liefde, W. (2011). *Lekgotla: The art of leadership through dialogue.* Second edition. Johannesburg: Jacana.

25 Kline, 1999.

26 De Liefde, 2011, p 24.

27 Du Toit, 2019.

28 Ibid, p2.

29   Ibid.
30   Ibid, p2.
31   Ibid.
32   Rosinski, P. (2003). *Coaching Across Cultures: New tools for leveraging national, corporate and professional differences.* London: Nicholas Brealey, p20.
33   Khoza, R.J. (2011). *Attuned Leadership: African humanism as compass.* Johannesburg: Penguin, p3.
34   Nussbaum, B., Palsule, S., and Mkhize, V. (2010). *Personal Growth African Style.* Johannesburg: Penguin.
35   Gafni, M. (2001). *Soul Prints: Your path to fulfilment.* New York, NY: Simon & Schuster.
36   Gafni, 2001, cited in Nussbaum, p46–47.
37   Schwab, K., and Davis, N. (2018). *Shaping the Future of the Fourth Industrial Revolution.* New York, NY: Currency, p1.
38   Schwab and Davis, 2018, p240.
39   Schwab and Davis, 2018.
40   Schwab and Davis, 2018.
41   Makho (2019). Personal interview. Johannesburg, 7 September.
42   Du Toit, 2019.
43   Ibid.
44   Ibid, p13.
45   Drucker, P.F. (2005). Managing oneself. (Reprint of article published in 1999.) *Harvard Business Review*, 10:2–14, p151.
46   Rød, A., and Fridjhon, M. (2016). *Creating Intelligent Teams: Leading with Relationship Systems Intelligence.* Johannesburg: KR Publishing.
47   Goleman, 1996, p149.
48   Parker, M. (2014). *It's Not What you Say, It's How you Say It!* London: Random House, p22.
49   Goleman et al., 2002a, p6.
50   Goleman, D., Boyatzis, R., and McKee, A. (2001). Primal Leadership: The hidden driver of great performance. *Harvard Business Review*, December, 79(11): 42–51.
51   Ibid, p44.
52   Goleman et al., 2002a, p6.
53   Goleman, 2006, p333.
54   Stout-Rostron, S. (2019). Theories, models and tools informing the High-Performance Relationship Coaching Model. In Stout-Rostron, S. (ed.), *Transformational Coaching to Lead Culturally Diverse Teams* (pp. 44–73). Abingdon, Oxon: Routledge, p61.
55   Goleman et al., 2002a, p38.
56   Ibid.
57   Goleman et al., 2002b, p63.
58   Goleman et al., 2001.
59   Kline, 1999, p101.
60   Ibid, p12.
61   Ibid, p36.
62   Ibid.
63   Kline, N. (2021). The Ten Components of a Thinking Environment, Worksheet, 2023.

64 Magadlela, D. (2015). The 'P' stance for leaders in meetings. *Business Essentials*, 10 September. URL: www.businessessentials.co.za/2015/09/10/the-p-stance-for-leaders-in-meetings/.

65 Magadlela, D. (2008). (Mis)understanding ubuntu: A reply. *Mail & Guardian Thought Leader*, 16 March. URL: thoughtleader.co.za/mis-understanding-ubuntu-a-reply/, p1.

66 Khoza, 2011, p10.

67 Pampallis, P. (2021). *Urban Hub 23 – Integral Africa: Thriveable Cities*. Cape Town: IntegralMentors, p17.

68 Khoza, 2011, p11.

69 Ibid.

70 Khoza, 2011, p12.

71 Magadlela, D. (2019). The case for Ubuntu Coaching: Working with an African coaching meta-model that strengthens human connection in a fast-changing VUCA world. In Stout-Rostron, S. (ed.), *Transformational Coaching to Lead Culturally Diverse Teams* (pp. 85–101). Abingdon, Oxon: Routledge.

72 Khoza, 2011.

73 Msila, V. (2015). *Ubuntu: Shaping the current workplace with (African) wisdom*. Randburg: KR Publishing.

74 de Liefde, 2011.

75 Ibid, p22.

76 Tutu, D. (1995). Nothing short of a miracle. In Thick, C. (ed.), *The Right To Hope: Global problems, global visions: Creative responses to our world in need* (pp. 1–4). London: Earthscan.

77 Hamel, G., and Breen, B. (2007). *The Future of Management*. Boston, MA: Harvard Business School Press.

78 Nobantu Coaching (2021). *Ubuntu Coaching for Coaches*. Training session dates: 6, 13, 20 and 27 March 2021. URL: nobantucoaching.co.za/services/.

79 Ibid.

80 Magadlela, D. (2020). Sawubona – "I see you": The understated power of greeting in coaching and human relationships. *COACH Magazine*, 31 August. URL: www.coach-magazine.com/sawubona-i-see-you/.

81 Kline, 1999.

82 Mpotulo, N. (2023). Personal interview. Johannesburg, 6 July.

83 Munyaka, S. (2023) Personal interview. Johannesburg, 5 July.

84 Kasonde-van den Broek, N. (2023). Personal interview. Johannesburg, 18 July.

Index

www.ingramcontent.com/pod-product-compliance
Lightning Source LLC
Chambersburg PA
CBHW062027210326

41519CB00060B/7194